The Magic
of
Finding Love and Peace

The Magic of Finding Love and Peace

By Tom and Caroline Lumbrazo

Copyright 2017 by Tom and Caroline Lumbrazo

Published by
When Angels Touch Publishing
1911 Douglas Boulevard # 85-140
Roseville, California 95661
916.782.8408

Design and printing by
Lorna Johnson Print!
Lorna@LornaJohnson.com and www.LornaJohnson.com

Printed in China

To order, go to www.whenangelstouch.com
or email Tom@whenangelstouch.com

ISBN: 978-0-692-88226-9

The Magic
of

Finding Love and Peace

Tom and Caroline Lumbrazo

Our Circle of Friends

Along the way on our 16-year journey, our Friends have been so instrumental in our success. They have given us great insights and information. They have also helped to provide the inspiration we needed to keep going through difficult times. They have guided and inspired us to go forward on our path. We honor them. This book is as much about them as us. You will see this as you read the various stories within this book. You will get to know the important roles that each of our Friends has played in our journey.

Emerald Alurin Stara ♥ Francie Marie ♥ Jaap van Etten ♥ Judith M. McLean, PhD ♥ Kathleen Scott ♥ Kerry Jehanne ♥ Mandy Milovich ♥ Linda Schooler ♥ Brook N. Rivera ♥ Alan Walden ♥

Dedication

Prior to 2001 and my terrible car accident with Archangel Michael saving my life, I did not really believe in Angels. I was like many people using their gifts of their five senses to navigate life on this third dimensional Earth each and every day. If you told me then that I would come to strongly believe in Angels in the future and to actually work with them, I would have to say you were crazy.

This book is about our life for the last 16 years and how we have embraced Angels and the Higher Realms of Existence. As a part of that growth, we had to rely on many people that somehow came to help us.

This book is dedicated to the many people and guides who have helped shape our lives. Our psychic friends have been integral to our survival and growth along this spiritual journey and our Archangels and other Spiritual Guides have helped guide and protect us through all the journeys on our spiritual path.

There is Linda Schooler, who we met in 2006. She predicted our immediate and long term futures with great accuracy. Emerald Alurin Stara who came to us in a vision in 2006. She is a wonderful tarot card reader and numerologist. Francie Marie came to us in 2007. She is so detailed in her accurate predictions and helps us to understand the Angelic and ET energies around us. Kathleen Scott came into our lives in 2007. She gives us wonderful healings for our bodies and also communicates with our loved ones who have passed, especially my Dad, John. Then there is Judith McLean, who has become a very special friend since 2010. While we have never met in person, she and I have communicated by email weekly since 2010. She has expertise in so many areas of spiritual development. She has been practicing in the spiritual field for nearly 40 years. We have also never met Jaap van Etten in person. He has been indispensible and has saved us many times from negative and evil energies around and attached to our bodies.

We also greatly appreciate our friend and cat and house sitter Brook Rivera. Without her, we would not have been able to travel so often or for so long.

We love them all. They are true friends with incredible talents. They genuinely strive to help others every day. Some are also listed under Spiritual and Intuitive Resources in this book, with more information about each one as well as contact information.

Of course, we owe everything to Archangel Michael. He awakened us and guided us all these years. We are also grateful for the other Archangels like Raphael, who has healed us, and Gabriel who has helped us create our four books. St. Anthony and St. Andrew came into our lives as well to guide us. All these and many other Angels and Guides are around us every day.

In addition, we want to dedicate this book to each other. We have always supported each other during our relationship over the last 50 years. Over the last 16 years, we have both strived to always be patient and loving. This was in spite of the many tests and challenges that were thrown at both of us. Our Love has endured and only grown stronger.

Caroline and I wanted to also dedicate this book to our precious cat, Tigger. He was 20 when he passed away. Tigger gave us great joy and happiness. He died during the last stage of the preparation of this book. He is still with us looking down with his Love. Here's to Tigger...

To all of them we send our Love and Gratitude!

Gratitude

A Guide to Reading this Book

This book is a compilation of true stories by the authors Caroline and Tom Lumbrazo. The book reflects their spiritual experiences since 2001.

The stories are primarily told by Tom from his perspective and therefore, the stories are told in the First Person by Tom. So when you see "I," this is Tom talking about the story he is presenting to you. Tom's wife, Caroline, will be mentioned as well in many of the stories as they both experienced many of the events together or worked together with regard to them.

You will see the names of Judith, Francie Marie, Linda, Kathleen, Alan, Jaap, and Emerald mentioned in the various stories. They are friends of Caroline and Tom who played an important part in their lives and helped them through the last 16 years of spiritual experiences and growth. Each of them is also listed in the "Intuitive and Psychic Resources" section of this book.

In the latter half of the book, there are photographs of clouds taken by Tom. These clouds are so unique and Tom and Caroline are pleased to be able to present them to you. Tom began taking cloud photos in 2007 and continues until the present time. Tom considers these photographs as messages to us to awaken to our spiritual selves. Tom has taken all of the cloud photographs. To make the images clearer, he has used color/contrast. None of them are PhotoShopped. He has attached the meditations to the photographs, which were created by Tom as well.

Also included in the book are some examples of Tom's artwork. They will be accompanied by titles or words of meditation.

Our stories, messages, memories, artwork, and photographs are our gift to all of you who read this book. We hope that you enjoy this book and it enhances how you perceive Love and Peace.

Table of Contents

Acknowledgements

Caroline and I feel it is important to honor the Creator of all things. We believe that whatever Creator you believe in, that Creator has manifested our very existence and the true meaning of our lives.

Many people throughout the world have been or are experiencing what might be called a "spiritual transformation." Many, like myself, have experienced this transformation after a Magical experience of a tragic traffic accident with an Angel by your side. Many of these people have written accounts or books on their transformation and what it might mean for others.

Caroline and I feel very blessed to have lived through the experiences of the last 16 years and now to be able to share them with you through this book, "The Magic of Finding Love and Peace." We hope that you find our book to be an inspiration for you to explore and to discover the Magic of the things you can see, and things that you cannot see.

We have many new friends over the last 16 years who have helped us weather the road of spiritual enlightenment. All of our friends are blessed with incredible intuitive talents. We have found them to be gifted, wise, giving, and loving. Without their guidance, our spiritual adventure since 2001 could never have happened. A very special "Thank You" goes to all of them including Alan, April, Emerald, Francie Marie, Judith, Kathleen, Linda, Brook, Jaap, Kerry, and Mandy. A very special "Thank You" goes to our book shepherd Lorna Johnson for her guidance, advice, and her incredible work on this book.

As you find in this book, Archangel Michael is mentioned frequently. He is the Angel that came into my Jeep prior to my vehicle accident and saved my life. He has been with me each and every day since. He has guided me in so many ways to make the right choices and to have the courage to explore this world and other realms of existence. I love him very much and have so much gratitude for all the things he has done for Caroline and I.

Foreword

by Judith M. McLean, PhD

No one can ever forget the wonder of childhood when we lay on our backs and watched the summer clouds floating overhead. We would call out to friends what we saw in the sky and compare notes as to what each saw in a particular cloud. A common thing we tended to see was "God on his throne," or cherubs. The sky was our nearest thing to actually seeing God in our youthful minds. But, as adults, we can recapture the wonder, excitement and nearness to Spirit as we once again lift our eyes on our walks and nature tours and experience all the splendor and wonder of clouds.

There will always be the skeptics who say that we project onto clouds what we want to see, much like the ink blot tests of psychologists. Maybe we do, or maybe Spirit just gives creation a nudge once in a while so we remember things beyond our daily lives. In this book, clouds have taken on the forms of angels. It is hard to find individuals who do not believe in angels and these wonderful cloud pictures of Tom's bring to mind the winged creatures of the Heavens. What could present a more soaring and inspirational picture than a cloud that brings to mind an angel looking over and down on us.

At times of sorrow and depression, anxiety and fear, nature is often the greatest healer. As we call out to Spirit in these times, "Mother Earth" and "Father Sky" often provide clues to our recovery. If we look up and see angelic forms in the clouds, we can believe there is something greater in our lives and that we are loved and cared for by invisible guardians. We don't have to be children to believe this.

Most of us imagine angels through the archetypal perspective of white luminous beings with wings, halos, flowing dresses, and harps of gold. However, the earliest creatures with wings of which we are aware came from Mesopotamian sculptures that later influenced Egyptian art and then Christian perceptions of guardian beings. Angels can appear to us in the usual stereotyped form or in other ways. Each person recognizes angels differently. Tom saw with his vision of St. Michael through the archetype of how Christian artists perceived St. Michael with his sword.

We may just see forms of light. Some people are not visionary and experience angelic forces through the hearing of a voice, thoughts or feelings.

In my own thirty-six years of spiritual pursuit, healing work, and clairvoyant experiences, I have experienced angelic forces in many ways. I think that angels can act through human beings or can appear in all kinds of forms. Angelic forces can radiate through animals. Deceased members of our family or ancestors can be our guardians. I remember one experience in a snow storm when my car got stuck in a deserted warehouse district at night. I could not get my car up the hill, which was icy. I kept trying to drive up the slope and slid right back down. This was before cell phones and I rapidly reached near hysteria. Suddenly I felt a gentle spirit slap across my face (like one would do to a hysterical person) and the words came to me telepathically to slowly try to drive up the hill again. This time I made it up the slope and safely reached home. This is an episode of angelic intervention that I will never forget.

Tom's spiritual experience of seeing a vision of St. Michael when he was in a car accident and later in the clouds set him on a journey that he never expected to take. Spirit chose a creative way to lead Tom into greater depths of spirituality and the ability to see God's messages in the clouds and through his remarkable art. We can all be grateful for Tom, his creative abilities, his skills in photography and most of all his love and willingness to share.

I have never met Tom in person, but we have a lively and ongoing email correspondence about everything spiritual. A mutual friend gave us each other's email addresses a few years ago at a time when we were both marketing our new books. I feel like I know Tom very well as he has shared his thoughts, visions, artwork, and cloud books with me. His generosity in giving to others shows his charitable inclinations and desire to share. He is a teacher of spirituality with his art and images as he helps our spirits to soar.

When you read Tom's fourth book "The Magic of Finding Love and Peace," take time with each story and photograph he presents. What does that story mean to you? What does the cloud form say to you? Does the book touch you inside? Does it stimulate you to take a rest and meditate? Do you feel the joy course through your inner being? This is a wonderful book showing how spiritual growth works. It may drive you to contemplate, and meditate - and especially pray. Treasure each story and photograph as a chance to take an inward journey and to be grateful for our magnificent lives. Say thanks to Tom each time you experience Creation and the Angels through his eyes!

My own transformation happened in 1980 when I was a member of the Church of Jesus Christ of Latter-day Saints. I had a spontaneous kundalini experience and the energy zoomed up my spine and left me clairvoyant, clairaudient, clairsentient, and with healing abilities. I had no reference point from which to understand what had happened to me with my Mormon acculturation. I also had a vision, much like Tom, at this time. A being of great light appeared to me and said he was a "savior" from another planet. Of course I could not comprehend that at the time and decided it must have been Jesus. But this being has been a guardian and guide to me for 32 years. He is my "angel." Other people have also had appearances of luminous beings who claim to be extra-terrestrial and there to help, teach and protect. So, again, angels come in many forms. My own story of transformation, angels, and ascension is told in the book below.

Reverend Judith M. McLean, PhD
Sanctuary11@comcast.net

Author of *Ascension Journey: A Handbook for Healing Through the Dimensions*

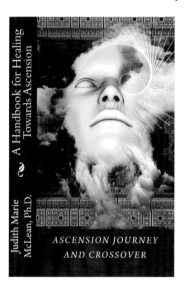

This book can be purchased on Amazon.com at the link below, through Kindle, Apple products, and from the publisher, CreateSpace.com.

http://www.ascensionjourney.com

Introduction

It is interesting how "The Magic of Finding Love and Peace" became our fourth book. In the fall of 2016, Caroline and I were running out of our third book, "Simply Angelic – Divine Images." So we agreed to reprint it with minor changes. As I sat down to make the minor changes, I was suddenly getting "messages" coming into my mind to expand the book in ways I had not intended. The messages were to include more cloud photographs, and to write the stories that tell of our spiritual journey since 2001. I am used to getting messages like this from the Angels around me so I always follow their guidance.

More messages came during an intuitive session with Kathleen. Kathleen began repeating what Archangel Michael and John, my Dad who had passed in 2011 and channels through her, were saying. They said to make this a much bigger book and include stories of the values and lives of the people in our country in the 1950s, to include conversations with my departed Dad and, of course, photographs of clouds. Then, our intuitive friend Alan from San Francisco, called me. He had not called for many months. Yet, he called to tell me that the Angels wanted me to be sure to include some photos of clouds from our previous three books in this new book. When I heard this same directive from our intuitive friend Alan, who is a respected channel and intuitive, there was no doubt what I had to do. It seemed that everyone was participating in directing the creation of this book and what it would convey.

This book is about the Magic in our world. It is about paying attention to the messages, synchronicities, and clues that are sent to us in so many ways. They are sent to us by Angels and others from the Higher Realms. It is about recognizing and following these messages, finding the path on which you are being led, and finding your purpose in this life. Now, you don't have to do any of this at all. It is your choice to listen or not listen. It is your choice to follow the messages or not. You have Free Will to decide either way. You may not believe that there are Angels or that they are assisting you in some way. That is okay!

This book is for all the people who might be interested in aspects of the spiritual subject in general. It is for people who might believe or who are not sure. It is also for people who do believe and have received messages of their own. Perhaps people who are on their own spiritual journey and are interested in how our journey has manifested will enjoy reading our stories. After 16 years, we have extraordinary and magical stories to share.

We have presented the stories in the best way we could. We have tried to detail all the aspects of each event or incident. We have even provided many photographs documenting many of these events. It is not our motive to make you believe these stories. We have provided you with all the evidence we have so that you can decide for yourself what you want to believe. Of course, there will be skeptics, and they have the right to choose to not believe any of these stories.

"The Magic of Finding Love and Peace" is a story of how Caroline and I have lived and evolved on a path of spiritual growth. We never intended this path. We were skeptics ourselves prior to 2001. We were happy in our normal human day-to-day existence. However, apparently there was another plan for us. On February 9, 2001, a new path unexpectedly began when I had a major vehicle accident on Highway 65 in Placer County, California. Seconds before the accident, a strong and loud male voice entered my Jeep. Much later, I came to understand that voice was from an Angel. In fact, it was the most powerful Angel, Archangel Michael. He directed me to slow to 35 from 60 which I did without hesitation. Seconds later, a vehicle pulled in front of me. Both vehicles were destroyed but we all survived with minor injuries. The policeman who came to the scene told me that I would certainly be dead if I had still been going 60. Without knowing it, we began new lives after that accident. For the next 16 years, everything changed for us. Everything!

Since then we have lived through challenges to our understanding of life, struggles to deal with what was happening to us, conflicts within each of us, and battles with invisible demons trying to influence or harm us. But we also have been so enlightened and filled with the Love and the Peace of the Angels. An Angel in human form, a woman I had never seen before, came to me for a moment in time two months after the accident. She told me calmly that my life would change dramatically and to journal every day or else I would forget. How did she know this? I could have easily told her to go away or ignored her advice. Somehow I knew she was delivering a very special message to me and I followed that message each day since the encounter. This has allowed us to be able to share with you the many stories in this book.

"The Magic of Finding Love and Peace" is a compilation of "magical" stories that have happened for us and to us. It is about finding the many new friends that have come into our lives and have helped us discover a path of spiritual enlightenment. These friends and our adventures over the last 16 years have guided us to discard many of the beliefs of our culture in favor of the many aspects of Love and of Peace.

We would have never thought this could happen to anyone, let alone Caroline and I. But it did and there is no turning back. The nature of the Energies of Love and of Peace are too strong to deny. Every day, something seems to happen around us that causes us to love our path even more. Every day, something amazing and tangible happens. For example, the day I opened our front door and standing at the threshold was a beautiful white pigeon. That pigeon immediately walked in like he lived in our home. He stopped in our small tiled entry, looked around, and then calmly turned around and walked out the door. He continued to walk down our walkway to the public sidewalk and he turned left and followed the sidewalk. Now you have to say that does not happen every day. We knew he was delivering a message just for us. The message was to stay at home and enjoy our life at home after our many international travels.

"The Magic of Finding Love and Peace" is a compilation of the events that happened to Caroline and I since 2001, and they are presented generally by the type of subject matter. This way you might be able to appreciate how and by whom the messages and events come to us. You will find many of our stories involve our new friends that have been sent by the Angels to us to help us along the way. We want to point out that our path has been frustrating as well. From 2001 to 2009, I became very frustrated with the process of this journey. So many things were happening that were emotionally painful. I was so frustrated and even somewhat angry. When I met my psychic friend Francie Marie in 2008, I asked her "Can you access your Angels and find out what is the ending of my journey?" A few seconds later, she said "They are saying you have to read the entire book to find out – you cannot read the last chapter first!" I said to her in response, "I guess they told me!" What is funny about this is that often I read the last page or last chapter of a book I am reading before reading the book. They knew this, didn't they?

Later in 2009, I was still so very frustrated. I met with Francie Marie again and I asked her to ask her Angels this question. "What if I wanted to stop being on this spiritual journey? What if I just wanted to lead a normal human existence again?" The Angels immediately responded through her and said "Think of a big dam and all the water behind it in the form of the reservoir. And then think of all the terrible destruction downstream if the dam busted… this could happen to you!" Well, that answer shook me up a bit. It was clear that there was no going back. I did not want to face something bad happening to Caroline or myself. After that message, I never looked back.

Year by year, more information was being given to us. It clearly was a well managed effort by the Angels to bring us along slowly so we didn't freak out about all the things happening to us.

During the 2000s, our belief systems were being constantly challenged. For a period of time from 2004 to 2009, Caroline and I were attacked by the unseen…by ancestral spirits, family members that had passed, even the powerful Djinn. These attacks were unsettling and frightening and they could come at any time. It was a frustrating period of time because how do you fight and win against things you cannot see.

Luckily, we were able to find several psychics that were so talented. They helped to guide us through all this. They were able to tell us what was happening to us. They predicted our futures with incredible accuracy. Linda, Francie Marie, Kathleen, Emerald, Jaap, Alan, and Judith became our resources and guides to assist us through the maze of spiritual challenges and growth. They became our very good friends as well.

Despite all these challenges, we persisted and persevered. We were determined to see this to the end or our end if that is what it took. Our motto was: if need be, we would go down trying – as at times it seemed our lives were being threatened. We would not give in to the evil of the other side. We felt like the salmon returning to its river to spawn with all those obstacles and dangers like the rapids, bears, and the fishermen that it has to face to survive. Over the years, we found people to help us understand all this and even to remove these evil spirits. Again, more growth and understanding about how this new path works.

We discovered we had to have patience. We found out that if we persevered and adopted a policy of patience, all things would work out eventually. This was a profound thing to learn… yet it was so simple and it worked. In addition, we had to always be positive in our outlook and to Love each other every day. Instead of breaking us apart, this evil actually made us closer in our relationship. We learned that Love truly conquers. Love is the antidote to all the negativity and evil that was around us, be it human or otherwise.

Through our trip to Peru in 2007, I began a journey with the clouds, so to speak. I saw my first incredible clouds of the Inca…the Condor, Puma, and Snake. From then on, it seemed I resonated with clouds in a special way. In fact, the clouds were sending me messages that I could capture through my camera. Our first three books were about those clouds and the messages they bring us to awaken to that magic of this planet. Those books were "Journey to the Clouds," "Faces of the Universe," and "Simply Angelic." This book also has many cloud images for you to digest and to see for yourself how very special they are.

This book is about synchronicities, clues and messages. An example of the synchronicity of a real life event and then a cloud image occurring was the day a hummingbird came to our home. It landed on the arm of our outdoor furniture. I walked slowly toward it and held out my right hand next to it. It did not quickly fly away as hummingbirds do. Incredibly, it actually climbed

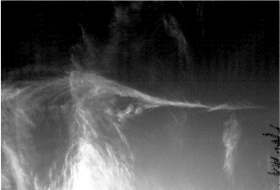

up into my hand and stayed for a minute. That same week, I saw a Hummingbird Cloud image in the sky and was able to photograph it.

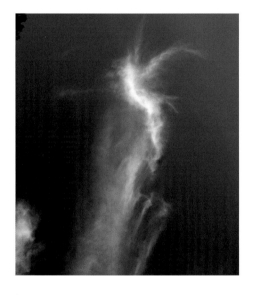

Another example of this kind of synchronicity was when I was sitting in a chair on our outside deck at about 4 in the afternoon. I just closed my eyes a second to relax, and suddenly I saw a white fairy hovering about a foot in front of my face. It looked like the one you might have seen as Tinker Bell in the movies. We live near a creek and fairies are said to live near water. So you see, fairies are real but we just cannot see them until they want us to. Again, a symbol of the magic around us all. I guess the fairy was just checking me out to see if I was a threat to it or not. A few days later, I saw the image of a fairy in the form of a cloud and I photographed it.

The magic never stops. One just has to recognize it. On 11/11/2011, while in Monument Valley and Sedona, Arizona, two more Angels in human form came to visit us. They made us promise to research the information that they showed us. It was about the meaning of Divine Love – the meaning of life for all of us. You can read this story and many more in this book.

All the while Caroline and I were growing through this journey, our bodies and minds were changing. In some cases it was not something we did consciously. For example, I lost my desire for any alcohol or beer whatsoever in 2012, and I have not had a drink since. Caroline also was affected to some degree. Also in 2012, something inside both of us made us realize that we had to remove all forms of negativity from our lives. Negativity was repulsive to us. The negativity on TV or movies, or within our group of friends and family, or even in the places we might visit. It all needed to be removed. Thinking about such things happening to us made us realize that we were indeed purifying our minds and bodies. I think that such purification allows more growth of our spiritual selves. As a result, I think even more incredible things happened for us since 2012.

This spiritual path that we have been led on has helped us to realize that we have been experiencing something very special. We wish everyone could share in this sort of experience.

This book is our attempt to share our story with you. A story of Karma, Past Lives and Reincarnation, Healing, how Numbers are so important, the Power of Crystals, discovering Orbs and other Life Forms on this planet, how Visions became a way of life, talking with Deceased Family Members, Clouds as Messengers, and truly discovering the Meaning of Life. You may resonate with some of our stories. Most of the time when we share our stories with other people, we find that those people have experienced similar magical things also, but seem too afraid to discuss them openly or to act on them.

Looking retrospectively, we could have made the decision NOT to go along with any of this spiritual path. When that Angel spoke to me in my Jeep in 2001, I could have totally ignored what he said. Perhaps I would have died at that very moment because I would not have reduced my speed. None of the last 16 years would have happened for me. So I feel it is a choice whether to explore the unknown or not. It is a choice to have that courage and to trust to adventure into something that you have no idea where you are going but you sense it is the right thing to do.

Each day in our lives all of us have to make choices from the simple to complex. Some are easy and simple, others are complex and so very difficult. Sometimes we have to step outside of the pressures put on all of us to conform. Think about the suggestions to us from TV shows and the many advertisements, or the people around us that want us to act a certain way. Or even the peer pressure from our friends that starts early in life. But we all have some measure of freedom to choose. I feel it is particularly important whether to decide to align and associate with the negative or the positive things in life. Do we hang out with the negative people who endeavor to control or hurt others? Or do we strive to improve ourselves with education and skills that would allow us to help others and ourselves? Do we make the conscious choice to contribute selflessly in a meaningful way to other people, and to society and the world? I am sure you know people that are negative or even evil? And you know people that are positive, strive to excel in life, and give of themselves to help others. From our perspective, those are the clear choices.

We firmly believe we have been put on this Earth to experience life on a beautiful planet with all its opportunities, challenges, pain and dangers. We are here to learn and help others. We are here to be stewards of this planet and to help it survive with all its inhabitants. Quite a responsibility! Each of us is challenged to do our part. Or we have the selfish choice to take from others and from the planet. Yes, I think our time on Earth is a test. It is a test of our resolve to find and live a life of Love and Peace.

So how does one try to start on a path of spiritual development? We think the first thing is to slow down and stop at times to reflect. Even for just five minutes. We are all very busy in our lives, work, home, driving, and using phones, computers, and computer games. But it does not take much time or effort to purposely slow down. When you are walking somewhere, survey the landscape around you and think about the gift of all the life that is there. It does not take much to stop and sit down and take it all in and analyze in your mind the beauty around you...a tree, a park, even the creations of humans. Getting in touch with your inner self during these times of reflection is so important. It allows you to determine if you are living the life you want or to question that life. It allows you to take in the amazing truth of why you are here on this planet. It allows you to question is there a God and who is it and why. It allows you to question how you and this planet got here. It allows you to question your entire existence here.

We have gone through all those moments. As we questioned, slowed down, stopped, we started to see the world in such a more valuable way. That pause allowed us to actually connect and listen to the Angels around us. Meditation also helped us to see that the Angels are there for each one of us. In my case, they shared with me hundreds of visions of all sorts of things, to guide us to places around the world to gain more experiences, and to ultimately find the meaning of life. We could not have done this without them.

There is no doubt in our mind that the meaning of life is to Love. Love of oneself. Love of others. Love of the planet Earth, our home. Love of all the life that abounds here and to honor that life. We human beings are a big puzzle piece in the puzzle called Earth. But it seems our puzzle piece is still trying to find that space in which we fit so that the puzzle is complete.

We hope our book inspires you to take the time for yourself, to pause and stop to reflect and discover your true self. Each of us has incredible power to shape our lives, and to shape the world around us. Through Love and Inner Peace so much can be created. We hope that you can find the Love of all of creation...Divine Love. It is there for each of you to discover it and live it.

Open Your Heart and You Will See!

Caroline   *Tom*

Love

About the Authors

Tom Lumbrazo is an author, photographer, city planner, and artist. Tom has a background in government and spent 40 years as a City Planner, and as a Planning Consultant in the Sacramento, California region.

In 2001, he had a life-altering experience during a major car accident. Seconds before the accident, a strong male voice spoke and directed him to slow from 60 mph to 35mph. Tom listened to this guidance immediately, and by going 35mph, his life was saved. Since that accident, his life has changed dramatically, leading him into the fields of photography, art, and writing. He has traveled extensively along with his wife Caroline to Egypt, Peru, Australia, Hawaii, Caribbean, Mexico, Ireland, England, France, and Italy. Along with this change in life interests, Tom has also gained the ability to see messages in such places as clouds, rocks, and sidewalks. He has had hundreds of visions as well. Through the psychics he uses, he is able to communicate with the Higher Realms of consciousness.

Caroline Lumbrazo spent her career working in libraries. Since childhood, books and reading have always been a significant part of her life. Travel and exploring new places and cultures, either by reading about them or planning travels to far away places has opened a new chapter in her life. Adventures and the travels that are described in the stories and photos in this book have been like a dream come true for her. Changes in her life over the last few years, and Tom's new interests, have given her a new perspective on life and many new interests to explore and follow. As she has grown from these experiences, she decided on her 65th birthday in Sydney, Australia, that she would no longer be Carol and from then on she would be Caroline, with a new focus and image.

You can see more photographs of our travels and many stories as well on our website.

How to contact the authors...

By email: Tom@whenangelstouch.com or Carol@whenangelstouch.com

By mail: When Angels Touch LLC, 1191 Douglas Boulevard #85-140, Roseville, CA 95661

Phone: 916.782.8408 | Website: Whenangelstouch.com | Facebook: When Angels Touch Facebook

Collage of Tom and Caroline

Who would have thought a boy of 3 in New York state and a girl of 3 from California would end up meeting in 1966 in Roseville, California and that they would be together for over 51 years?

Who would have thought that Tom and Caroline would be able to see their favorite team in 2010 — the San Francisco Giants — win the World Series for the first time since 1954?

Who would have thought Tom and Caroline would swim with the Dolphins and travel the world in search of Archangel Michael, and Love, and Peace?

All Things are Possible!

The Lion is Tom's Spirit Guide

I have been attracted to cats, tigers, and lions all my life. I have had so many cats as pets since I was very young. I guess I was always attracted to their independence and peace. I was also attracted to their cleanliness and their efforts to groom themselves each day. For the most part they are quiet, peaceful beings. All that appealed to me.

As I got into the spiritual side of things, I quickly learned of my infatuation with Lions. I thought about my past and how even as a child I had to watch lions on TV. When going to the zoo, I remember it to be such a treat to see the lions. I learned more recently that there are reasons for this attachment.

In delving into my past lives through sessions with psychics, I learned that very possibly I was a lion in a past life. I was surprised to learn that many people have past lives as animals. In addition, it is very possible I had past lives in ancient Rome where lions were used and killed in the Coliseum. It was also possible that I was in the Coliseum as a human slave or Gladiator and encountered the Lions.

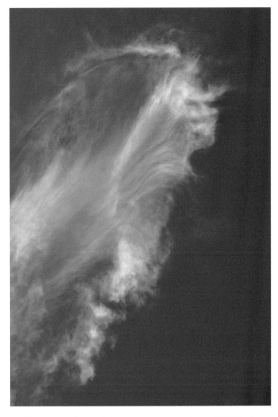

I am fascinated how I must see movies with lions in them. The most emotional movie for me is "Gladiator" with Russell Crowe. Each time it is on TV, I am compelled to see it. Somehow that movie brings me back to those times when I might have lived. I don't cry when I see movies, but each time I see that movie, I cry. How do you explain it other than that there is some connection. I feel this connection deep inside me.

I believe very strongly that the Lion is my Spirit Guide. Often, a spirit guide gives you the aspects of personality of that animal. In the case of the Lion, it has the personality traits of courage, personal strength, self confidence, and assertiveness. As I have grown with my spiritual journey, I have been keenly aware of these traits within me. Just take courage. I have had to exhibit courage many times in fending away evil spirits attached to me. Or to be courageous enough to be very public with the incredible things I have seen or experienced and share them with people.

Perhaps you have an affinity with an animal that could be your spirit guide just like me.

The Raven is Caroline's Spirit Guide

Encounters with Ravens have fascinated and attracted us over the last several years. During this time of spiritual encounters and journeys that we have taken, Caroline has been especially drawn to Ravens and she considers the Raven as her spirit guide. I can understand why, as she seems to have aspects of a Raven personality. We often kid each other when we are taking our daily walk. Because if she sees something shiny on the ground, she most always has to pick it up and take it home to store with her other Raven-like possessions.

Caroline also feels like the Raven Spirit has been with her in her past lives, particularly as a connection to her Celtic past life.

According to the book "Animal Spirit Guide" by Steven D. Farmer, the appearance of Ravens means that magic is in the air and something special is about to happen. That has surely been the case with many of the encounters that we have had with Ravens. Ravens are a very spiritual creature. Legends and stories about them abound in many cultures around the world. The behavior of Ravens has been studied, and it is our understanding that Ravens have been proven to have great intelligence. They have greeted us on many of our trips to sacred sites such as Stonehenge in England, the Grand Canyon, Hendaye in France, and in Canada.

The most amazing of these encounters was at Stonehenge in a driving rain storm. We were just concluding our visit when eleven Ravens landed in a group on the grass between us and the huge stones. Imagine that these Ravens were flying around us in that driving rain storm, and yet instead of taking cover, they landed near our feet. They began to chatter in a language that sounded almost human. It clearly was not Raven language. They seemed to want to tell us something before we left. We felt like they were making sure that we spent just a few more minutes near the stones before we had to leave for the bus.

On another occasion, in Hendaye, France we arrived by train and started to walk around the town in order to locate a place to stay for the night. Little did we know that it was still off season and there was very little open. In fact, we walked for at least two hours and could not find one hotel that was open. We were very tired! Suddenly, a Raven swooped down over our heads and made a quick right turn down a small street. We decided that was a sign, so we followed him. Sure enough, there was an open hotel at the end of the block with a lovely room waiting for us. As far as we were concerned, that Raven read our minds and found out that we desperately needed a hotel. He definitely helped us.

Then there was the story of how we bought a large Raven sculpture from a local artist. Before we purchased that Raven, he and his wife told us that the price was $3,000. They also told us that they needed the money that very day as it was critical to making the last payment for the adoption of a baby for their daughter. If the money was not delivered, the months-long process for adoption would be cancelled. So the Raven, even in sculpture form, was magically involved in this adoption of a baby.

Each time we encounter Ravens, either in real life or in the many art works that we have been drawn to and often acquired, we have felt that we have gotten a message from them. Our home is filled with images of the Raven and we often wonder what message they will impart to us next and what magic they will bring into our lives.

One of the legends of the Raven is of bringing knowledge and light to the world...as expressed in the following story "The Box of Daylight":

"Raven, the Trickster, was walking along the beach, it was the beginning of time. The world was dark. The sun, moon, and stars were kept in boxes by a wealthy old man who lived with his beautiful daughter at the Headwaters of the Nass River. The Fishermen of the Night told Raven about the treasures, and he hurried to the house of Nass Shaak Aankaawu.

Raven transformed his spirit into a tiny spruce needle, which the young woman swallowed when she drank. She became pregnant and gave birth to Raven in the form of a human child.

Like all grandfathers, old Nass Shaak Aankaawu loved his little grandson, and he gave him anything he asked for to play with. So when the child asked to play with the stars, moon and sun boxes, one by one the old man gave in to him. When nobody was looking, Raven opened the boxes, and the precious objects inside flew out through the smoke hole and up into the dark sky.

But there was still no light in the world. Raven turned himself back into his bird form again, and took the final box, the one they call the Box of Daylight. He flew back to the river where he opened the box, and broke daylight over the Fishermen. They became frightened and they ran away and hid. They became the creatures of the night.

But the rest of the human beings looked around and they saw their world clearly for the first time. And they marveled."

One of the many versions of "The Box of Daylight" legend as told by the Naa Kahidi Theater. The legend and other stories about ravens can be found in "Ravensong: A Natural and Fabulous History of Ravens and Crows" by Catherine Feher-Elston, 2005.

Watch for Ravens to appear in your life. If you are alert to the messages of the Raven, you might encounter the magic and special wisdom that they can bring to you and to this planet.

Perspective by the Authors

We, the authors Tom and Caroline, believe it would be helpful to understand our perspective on our existence here on Earth. We have experienced many incredible things over the last 16 years. As a result, our knowledge of our world, the universe, and the spiritual elements has grown dramatically.

We have come to understand that all of us on Earth are Energy. Everything is Energy in the universe. By the laws of physics, Energy cannot be destroyed. We understand that there is at least one universe and probably many more. Many scientists are now saying there are multiple universes and many dimensions of existence.

These scientists understand that we and our Earth are in the Third Dimension...A Dimension of solid objects. Additionally, quantum scientists now theorize that there may be as many as 12 or 13 Dimensions of existence or consciousness. We also believe that other intelligent life forms live in these higher dimensions.

We also believe that each of us has a Soul, including animals as well. We believe that our human bodies are the vehicle by which our Soul travels on the Earth each day. And that when the body weakens and dies, the Soul survives and lives on through eternity. The Soul may then reincarnate many times in other human bodies on Earth and perhaps on other planets. We believe that the reincarnation process is one by which we learn lessons of existence, karma, and Love.

We believe in a force that created all that exists here and in the universe. That loving force is God or the Creator Being mentioned in religions. It may be called Source as well.

We feel we must honor this Creator and have gratitude for everything created. That loving force likely created intelligent life on other planets.

We also believe in Angels. We feel the many kinds of Angels are guides and messengers for us if we listen carefully. They help us on our path through life on Earth. But, it is each human being's right to Free Will to make decisions that may or may not agree with the Angelic Guidance.

We believe in good and evil and positive and negative energies. We believe that such things exist in all the dimensions and that we each have to make our own personal decisions about which path we select and live...Good or Evil or Positive or Negative.

We believe in magic. Magic has been used throughout history to make what seems to many the impossible, possible. It can be used for either good or evil.

As weird as it may sound, we believe that Earth is very important to the struggle in the Higher Realms of the battle of Light and Dark forces. We believe that each of us can help the

Light forces in these Higher Realms through our spiritual growth and always having LOVE in your Heart.

Last and maybe the most important, we believe that the meaning of life here on Earth for each of us is LOVE. It is about understanding and living a life centered on Divine Love. Sounds simple, but we believe it takes work to put your mind and body in a state of Love each and every day. But it can be done. We practice it each day and it makes our life so much more meaningful and enjoyable.

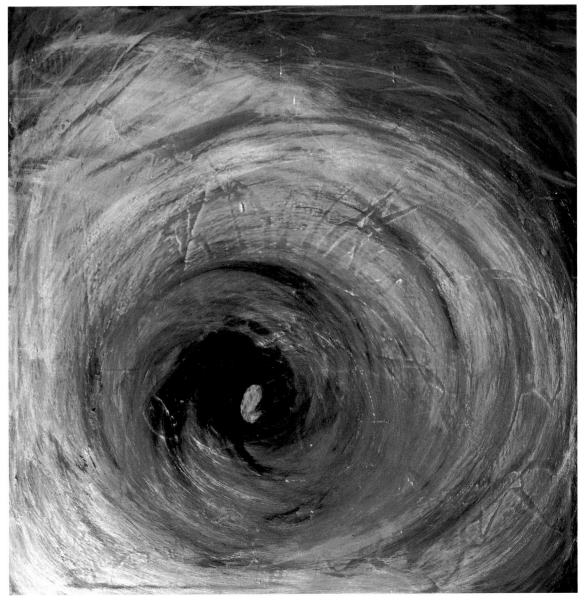

Awakening

Chapter 1

Archangel Michael Introduces Himself

The Angel Came Knocking and Everything Changed Forever

I will never forget the date of February 9, 2001! On that day, my life and the life of my wife Caroline changed forever. It was that day at noon when I was driving home on Highway 65, a four lane expressway, in Placer County, California that a strong male voice shouted out from the passenger seat area of my Jeep and said "SLOW TO 35!" I looked around in my car and of course there was nobody. Instantly, I felt I had better listen to that voice. I slowed to 35 from 60 mph. Seconds later, a car with three young men passed and went to the traffic signal up ahead and stopped at the GREEN signal. Yes, they stopped at a green light! I began to wonder what they were doing. As I approached them in the opposite lane, they immediately turned to the left and stopped perpendicular to my oncoming Jeep. I had no space to avoid them and as a result, hit their car on the left front side. My Jeep jumped up on their hood and both vehicles were pushed forward together into the intersection. Both vehicles were totaled. I was injured on my legs, some of my ribs were severely bruised, and my head had hit the steering column. My life had changed all in a split second but I am still alive!

When the California Highway Patrol came to investigate, I told the officer of that voice and what it said to me. He responded, "Sir, you would have surely died at 60 mph, I see it all the time!" At that moment, I knew I had been given a chance to live. But why?

Two months later, a woman came to me while I was at a public event. She quickly told me that my life would change and that I must journal the daily events or else I would forget them. Then she left abruptly. I had never met her before but in retrospect, she was right. Now, I firmly believe she was an Angel in a human body sent to deliver that message.

After months of healing, I began to investigate this voice. Who was it who came into my car and spoke? I could not forget it. I went to psychics of all kinds. They were not helpful in finding that answer. I had to wait until 2005. One night around 1:30 a.m., my wife Caroline and I were instantly awakened when our entire bed was being lifted about a foot into the air and dropped onto the floor. Several times! At the same time, our bedroom lights went off and on, including one that was not plugged in. All this happened for about 20 seconds. We, of course, were stunned. Our immediate reaction was that someone was in our house. I got up and checked but everything was locked.

As we settled down, Caroline and I talked about it and tried to figure it all out. We had no answers. Then as I tried to sleep, I closed my eyes for a brief second, and instantly, I had my first vision ever. It started like the old TVs. When you turned on the old TVs of the 1950s, the screen started with a bright dot of white light in the center and then that expanded out to the full screen. That bright light in my vision expanded out into the image of a huge Angel standing

perpendicular to me and looking right at me. Even today, I cannot provide the words that would adequately describe the beauty and color of that Angel. The Angel then changed to an image of him on a horse with sword and shield. He was looking right at me. Then it was done.

I had a hard time with all this as I really did not believe in Angels prior to my accident. In this life, I dealt with things that I could see, smell, and touch. But I also knew that something weird was happening to us.

The next morning I felt compelled if not pushed to go to the bookstore and look up Angels. I picked the first book with Angels written on the side of it. I pulled it out and randomly opened to somewhere in the middle. Unbelievably, there was a drawing of that Angel I just saw in my vision! It was identified as Archangel Michael, the most powerful Angel of all! He was on his horse with that sword. Now I knew what I was dealing with! Still, the lingering question of why was all this was happening to me.

Shortly after the bed incident, I started to have an unbelievable craving to play George Michael music. I had to play it all the time. I had to play it on my drive to work and back and during my time at home. Each and every day I had to have that music. After some thought, I understood I was being protected by Archangel Michael. It was Archangel Michael saying he was with me.

Then there were the attacks. From 2004 through 2010, I was being attacked by negative or evil entities and I did not know why. At times, I could see them or hear them. They seemed to be trying to take control of my body and mind. Sometimes I felt like I had one or two other people inside of me trying to disrupt my personality or make me physically do something. Later I found out from an intuitive person in the Sedona, Arizona area, Jaap van Etten, that these were ancestral spirits and other negative beings including the powerful Djinn. So now I knew why Archangel Michael was trying to protect me. Fortunately, Jaap was able to remove these negative beings remotely from Sedona, but it took several sessions over the years. All of that was a learning experience about how to deal with the evil that is on this planet and also in the Higher Realms of existence.

In 2008, Caroline and I had our visible proof of Archangel Michael. We were in Sedona walking an outdoor labyrinth at the St. Andrews Episcopal Church when the clouds swirled overhead and suddenly the image of the Angel showed on his horse and with sword. I took photographs of it. It has become my most treasured cloud image. Now I had my proof that I could show anyone that I was not completely crazy.

It would take another separate book to detail all the little things that happened over the 16 years and how Archangel Michael was involved in all of them. We marveled at the fact that he seemed to be with us each day through these little things he did. Eventually, I got into meditation on a daily basis, even if it was only for five or ten minutes. That led to me being able to connect with Archangel Michael. We were able to develop a form of communication through the use of Light. If I asked a question, he would respond with a Light flashing in my vision to indicate that the answer was yes. I learned that if the Light was very bright, it signaled that the answer was a very significant or important yes. If there was no Light, then the answer was no. So we had developed a language using a code.

Also, I would always see his presence whenever I closed my eyes. Before the 2005 event with the bed raising, I would always see black when I closed my eyes. After that, I was seeing a violet or deep purple color. Upon researching colors of the various Archangels, I learned that a deep and vibrant violet color was representative of Archangel Michael's presence. I was able to capture that when Caroline and I went to Ireland in 2013. We were taken by our tour guide to an ancient Celtic cemetery and Caroline took a photograph of the guide and myself. Over my head was this brilliant violet color indicating Archangel Michael was with us even there.

Every night I would close my eyes to go to sleep. But immediately, I would see swirls of beautiful violet light. Sometimes they would come from deep in my vision and seemingly form clouds of violet and come rapidly towards me and envelope my head. Other times, these clouds of violet would emanate from my head area and fly out until I could see them no more. These images would last for as long as I was awake. Sometimes it was hard to sleep as these colors were so beautiful. It all felt so comforting.

Whenever I am in a session with a psychic, the psychic immediately says Archangel Michael is in the room with us. This happens all the time and it is meaningful in that the psychic knows nothing about me yet feels the presence of the Angel. It seems that Archangel Michael has guided us through each day from the time of my accident.

This book, "The Magic of Finding of Love and Peace," is about a process of Discovery. It is about what has happened to Caroline and I over the last 16 years. In truth, it is about Archangel Michael and how he has entered and shaped our lives. It is about how he has sent us nearly around the world to visit ancient sacred sites. It is about how he has sent us to retrace places of our past lives. Most importantly, he has guided us to learn and understand the various types of Love. He has definitely opened our minds to Divine Love...the Love of all things created by God or whatever Divine Being you might believe in.

Over the last 16 years, we were guided to discover the world and the natural and spiritual laws that govern it. If we didn't get the message to travel someplace, another sign would be given to us to make sure we heard it and agreed to do it. Once we arrived in a foreign country, we were led to find why we were here. For example, we were guided to go to England and

France in 2008, 2013, and 2014. It was clear that the Angels wanted us to see Stonehenge and Glastonbury Tor in England and especially to learn about Ley Lines.

Ley Lines are the underground energy lines or grid of the planet Earth. You can actually feel the electrical type energy flowing under the planet in certain locations such as in nearby Avebury. The ancient people all over the world knew about this energy and built their churches, cathedrals, and other important buildings on top of them. We also learned of the Archangel Michael and Mary Lines. They are also ley lines. Over the years we were definitely guided to visit such sites and locations where the Michael Line traversed. In many of these places, there were reports of Archangel Michael actually being seen over the centuries.

The Michael Line stretches from the west side of Ireland, through the southwestern part of England, then into the entire length of France, then diagonally traveling through Italy and ending in Israel. Over the years, we have been to various locations over that ley line.

Another Discovery came in 2007 in Peru. I was presented with the remarkable clouds of the Inca Gods...the Condor, the Puma, and the Snake that I explained in the Introduction. I was so impressed with seeing these clouds that it became an obsession. In a sense the clouds were talking to me through images of people, animals, insects, and alien beings. It seemed I especially resonated with them. The more I looked, the more I saw. It seemed that the clouds had consciousness.

I had so many outstanding and unique cloud photographs, I ended up doing three books on them... "Journey to the Clouds" in 2009, "Faces of the Universe" in 2010, and "Simply Angelic" in 2013.

Each book I drafted was with the help of Archangel Michael and Archangel Gabriel, who is the Messenger Angel. Archangel Michael would systematically wake

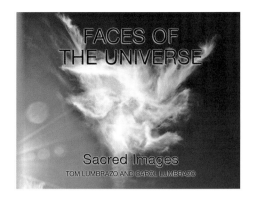

me up at 1:30 a.m. each early morning. He wanted me to work on the book several hours each day and then I could go off to work the rest of the day. I learned that if I did not get up, he would not let me sleep until I did. I realized that was the only way the books would get done as I was working full-time.

After the book that was published in 2013, Archangel Michael woke me up at precisely 6:00 a.m. one morning and he said or put these words into my mind... "Send this book to all places named St. Michael!"

After thinking about it, it seemed so right to send "Simply Angelic" to those people more likely to understand Archangel Michael and spiritual enlightenment. So that day I started and have continued that distribution throughout the world.

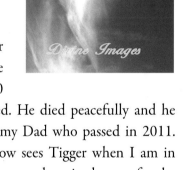

This book will guide you through some of the most amazing things that Archangel Michael has shown us or that we experienced. Generally, we have arranged the stories according to the subject and also chronologically.

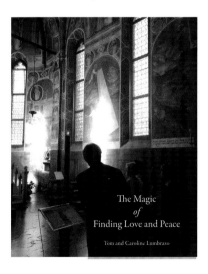

The events for us don't ever seem to stop. In the last stage of writing this book, our 20 year old cat named Tigger died. He died peacefully and he ascended instantly to be with my Dad who passed in 2011. My psychic friend Kathleen now sees Tigger when I am in session with her. He sends his Love and gratitude to us for the time we had together on Earth.

The Sword of Archangel Michael
Appears in Our Neighborhood

One late winter afternoon in February 2011, Caroline and I decided to go on a long walk in our neighborhood. A storm had just passed through our area and there were many clouds still above us. After about an hour, we approached the intersection that is situated a couple of blocks from our home.

I noticed some clouds straight ahead that appeared to be swirling. So I decided to take a photograph of them. I did not think much of those clouds other than their swirling effect. Two days later, I finally opened up that photograph on my iPhone to look at it.

I could not believe my eyes! The photograph I took was just of the neighborhood street, houses, and the clouds above. Now looking at the photograph it showed something entirely different. It showed a very intense magenta color in the form of a rigid straight line coming from within the clouds all the way to the ground just in front of where we were standing.

I looked at the photograph some more to see if there was a refraction of light or color which sometimes you can get when taking photographs with some sunlight involved. But this was not the case. The line was too intense and rigid and so straight. Additionally, the line actually went in front of and behind the clouds and then came out again. I had never seen anything like that before. I was in awe of it! No doubt this magenta line was real. We could not see it with our eyes but the camera picked it up. We have had other incidents where a camera sees more than the human eye.

I was so excited about the photograph that I decided to show one of my psychics. I showed Francie Marie and she said her guides told her it was the Sword of Archangel Michael. I believe her as she has been pretty infallible in her predictions and interpretations. She taps into her guides quite well and they interpret for her.

I also consulted the internet about the spiritual meaning of magenta when it is presented to you. According to internet sources that explain the meaning of each color, Magenta means Universal Love at the Highest Level. Perhaps Love was being expressed by Archangel Michael. We have learned after 16 years of spiritual experiences that the Meaning Of Life is Love. So it all makes sense to Caroline and I. What do you think this Magenta line is?

The Synchronicity of a CD and Archangel Michael

Sometimes funny things can happen to you that just don't make sense. For instance, you think you get a glimpse of a person moving across your living room but there is nothing there. Or you experience a "déjà vu" feeling that you were in a certain place before but you cannot prove it.

Sometimes you get proof like I did in 2009. Caroline and I had been going to a shop called the Empress Shop in Placerville, California. A full story on this shop can be seen later in this book. After that first experience with the owner of the shop, we became somewhat friends and we came back to her shop several times. Then one day in 2009, we drove 45 minutes from our home to see her and perhaps buy something in her

shop. We drove into the parking lot and it was empty which was very unusual.

We got out of our car and proceeded to walk towards her building, then I spotted in the distance a silver flat object laying flat on the asphalt. As Caroline and I got closer we could see that it was a music CD. I told Caroline that someone has lost their CD or they just trashed it.

Now remember at this time, I was being somewhat fanatical about George Michael music. I had all his CDs and listened to him in the car or at home all the time. It was an obsession. I am sure Caroline was so tired of hearing the same thing constantly but I had to do what I was feeling inside of me. This went on from 2005 to 2010.

When I stooped over to pick up the CD, I just could not believe it! It was a CD of George Michael music. It was a copy of his "Ladies and Gentlemen" album. How in the world did this CD get here on this parking lot? There was no plastic cover to be seen in the area or any other CDs. Why a George Michael CD? Why not some other CD? So many questions come into mind when something like this happens.

It was such a synchronistic event for me personally since I was so into George Michael and Archangel Michael at the same time. I cannot give you a perfect explanation other than to say Archangel Michael wanted me to know that he was with me now wherever I go and at any time of the day or night. Possibly, he wanted to remind me to "Breathe, Believe, and Receive" which was the message from my first experience at Empress. What an impressive way to show his presence!

So you see there are so many ways that messages can come in for you. We believe that each one of us has an Angel or two around us who are happy to assist us. You just have to open your mind to the possibility that anything can happen. Many times these messages are very personal and are not for anyone else but you. So if it seems that you tell a friend of such an incident and the friend does not believe you or thinks you are crazy, it does not matter. What matters is that you understand and accept the message. Remember "Breathe, Believe, and Receive!"

Believe

SKELLIG
MICHAEL

ST. MICHAEL'S
MOUNT

MONT
ST. MICHEL

CHAPEL OF
ST. MICHAEL

CASTEL
SANT'ANGELO

MONTE
SANT'ANGELO

ARMEGGEDON,
ISRAEL

Archangel Michael Ley Line

The line connects the island of Skellig Michael on the west coast of Ireland, to St. Michael's Mount in southern England, to Mont St. Michel in northern France, to Castel Sant'Angelo in Rome, Italy to Monte Sant'Angelo near Bari, at the east coast of Italy, through Greece, and ending near Armageddon, Israel.

If you wish to find out more about the St. Michael Ley Lines, including maps of the locations of the ley lines, you can research it on the internet at www.ancient-wisdom.com/stmichael.htm

Pilgrimage to the Archangel Michael Ley Line and Sacred Sites

Over a period of several years, Caroline and I learned that we had been guided to travel internationally specifically to see the Sacred Sites on the Archangel Michael Ley Line. That line is energy flowing through the planet in a specific place. It runs generally from Skellig Michael on the west coast of Ireland, through the southern parts of England, then into and through France, through Italy, and ends at Armageddon, Israel.

In fact, in my very first meeting with my psychic Linda Schooler, she said I would travel to the American Southwest within six months, and then internationally the rest of my life. That was in 2006 and it all has turned out to be true. One hundred percent true! Quite unbelievable!

We would often get messages from Archangel Michael to travel to these sacred sites. We discovered that they were on the Archangel Michael Ley Line. It became obvious to us that there was a purpose for us to have to travel to these sites. The travels became a way of life for us. Each place we visited was a place that Archangel Michael was reported to have been seen over the centuries.

It is amazing to think of all these sites, but more amazing how many things have been named Archangel Michael, St. Michael, or Michael to honor this great Archangel. In England alone, I researched through the internet all the places named St. Michael and the total was 687.

In essence, Caroline and I have been on a Pilgrimage to visit and honor Archangel Michael over the last several years. In addition, we have followed the ley lines in the Earth, and other Sacred Sites. Each site is so special, filled with centuries of history and many with the energy of Archangel Michael.

The Archangel Michael Ley Line starts at Skellig Michael. It is an island out in the ocean just west of the Ireland coast. When the sea is generally calm, one can get a boat to the island.

Then traveling east to the southwest area of England, there are several sites including the Glastonbury Tor [St. Michael's Tower] in Glastonbury, and the Chalice Well in Glastonbury.

Further east is the well-known site of Stonehenge. As we walked into the center, a bolt of lightning jumped over our heads, with a thunderous roar. I can be seen in the photograph with the beautiful Orb in the center. Orbs seem to inhabit many sacred sites. Then further east is Avebury where the ley line is powerful with a large stone circle and the carved stone of Merlin.

Further south, there is the major site at St. Michael's Mount, an island just off the southern coast of Cornwall. The St. Michael's Church is on the top of this island.

In France right off the coast is Mont St. Michel. This huge castle-like structure is protected by the high tides each day. Then there is the site of Carnac, in the region of Brittany, with more than 10,000 huge stones aligned in row after row.

Further south is Paris with its many sculptures of St. Michael, fountains, and streets like Boulevard Saint Michel.

Going south, we also visited the unique town of Le Puy en Velay. This town has several small ancient volcanoes within it. On one of them at nearly 1,000 feet has the Chapel of St. Michael on top of it.

It is truly remarkable that a small chapel could be built hundreds of years ago on this very steep ancient volcano. It was quite a climb.

Traveling into Italy, we visited Rome with its Castel Sant'Angelo, a fortress-like structure with a large metal sculpture of Archangel Michael on its roof.

Further south along the Adriatic Sea coast is Gargano, Italy. High upon a small mountain is the Sanctuary of Monte Sant'Angelo, which is the world-famous site of the cave where Archangel Michael was seen many centuries ago. On top of the cave is the building and access to the cave.

We stayed in the St. Michael Hotel which lies on top of the cave. We could not sleep all night as the energy was so strong from the cave and St. Michael.

During our pilgrimages, we saw so many artist renditions of Archangel Michael. Many are centuries old. Here are a few from the Monte Sant'Angelo Sanctuary museum.

Caroline and I have also visited other Sacred Sites in the world that are situated on other ley lines. We started our journey in Peru in 2007 with its many sacred sites.

Then in 2008, we took our adventure to Egypt with its pyramids and many sacred temples.

In 2015, we traveled to Australia and visited Uluru, an ancient mountain that spikes right out of the outback desert in Australia. Uluru is a sacred site of the Aborigine peoples. It also is like Stonehenge in that many ley lines from around the world converge here.

More locally, there is Sedona, Arizona with its red landscape. This is where I was presented with the Archangel Michael Cloud over the St. Andrew Church and was able to take that photograph.

Our pilgrimages throughout the world have helped us grow and evolve spiritually. These sites carry great energies from within the planet. From our perspective, there can be no mistake that many of these special places are blessed with Archangel Michael energy and other ley line energies. Millions of people travel to these sacred sites each year to be near the special energies within them.

As I finished this story, I started singing the song "Moon River." I am sure my Dad channeled into me and sent me this song as it reminds Caroline and I of our many pilgrimages throughout the world.

Additional photographs of our travels can be found in our website www.whenangelstouch.com under the category of Sacred Journeys.

Spiritual Enlightenment

Chapter 2

Synchronicities, Visions, and Messages

_____

*Synchronicity is the ever-present reality
for those who have eyes to see.*

– Carl Jung

Vision of "Breathe, Believe, Receive"

I started to have many visions in 2006. Of course, I would document as many as I could in photographs and in a log book. Here is a story of deliberate guidance.

In the summer of 2006, we decided to take a three-day vacation to Lake Tahoe, which is about a two-hour drive from our home. On the Sunday night before we were to leave to go back home on Monday, I was awakened at 1:30 a.m. When I closed my eyes for a second, I saw a beautiful color fill my entire field of view. That color was a mixture of green and blue. In my mind, I was trying to figure out why I was given this color and what does it mean. Then the vision talked to me and said the color – AZURE! But why?

Now you have to understand that at this time, I was seeing a lot of visions. They would come when I was about to sleep, or in the middle of the night, or when I woke in the morning. I was also under a lot of strain and frustration about what was happening to me. What was happening to me?

I told Caroline at breakfast on Monday about the vision and she was amused. How could she really believe me? I am sure that during this time these things made her uneasy. What was going on with her husband of 36 years? After breakfast, we started to make our way home on Highway 50. As always, we have to stop somewhere in the middle of the trip for a pit stop at Starbucks. When we got off the freeway and entered the downtown of the foothill town of Placerville, we searched for the Starbucks. But as luck would have it, the downtown street was closed for repairs and we had to decide to turn around or find some parking right where we were on the main street.

That is when it started to get a bit interesting. There was a parking lot directly to the left of us. So we parked there. And of course, there was a café right next to the parking lot, so we could get an iced tea for Caroline. After getting the tea, we were walking out of the café and noticed that right next door was another shop which looked interesting. We got to the front entrance of that shop and the front door was open and guess what - the door was painted in an AZURE color. In addition, the door had handwritten phrases all over it in AZURE as well. The phrases were very poetic. The door even had part of a poem that read... "Azure Seas." As we saw that door color, we felt that we were being led to this very specific place through the AZURE guidance. So we went in. As we entered the store, we also noticed that all the shelving in the store had the same poetic handwriting in the AZURE color.

Now our interest was piqued. We met a very nice woman who was the owner of the store. By the way, the store was named Empress. We asked her what was with all the azure color and the writing on the door and in the store. She said in college she was into a famous poet and thought putting some of his poems in her store would add something special. She added that when she bought the store, she wanted to put things she loved in it. The store had all kinds of things for purchase such as clothes, CDs, statues, and jewelry. Caroline and I decided to look around the store to see if there was any other message in there for us. Or was this adventure just for us to meet her. We looked at every little thing in the store.

After about twenty minutes of looking around, Caroline declared from across the room "I think I found it!" When I went over to her, she said "Look at the paintings in this small box!" So I went through these paintings in cellophane wrapping and about 12 by 14 inches in size. As I got through about ten of them, then there it was! A small print with the entire background in AZURE! But there was more. Imagine in your mind that Azure background to the painting with a large white Angel in the center with wings spread, and above it were the words, "Breathe, Believe, Receive" and then the words "It's All Happening" on her abdomen. It was a perfect message for us at that time in our lives encouraging us to continue on our spiritual path.

We bought that print and it hangs in my home office as a reminder of the guidance that occurred that day and the spiritual journey that Caroline and I have lived since. The message rang true for us. So many spiritual things have happened to us, many of them beyond belief. Often little events like this and following the clues that are given to us often result in such a positive experience like this one.

Over the years, more experiences have occurred that involve this same message. This image has appeared to us on greeting cards and at other times, often when our "belief" was being tested.

But what if we had not followed the clues? What if we had closed our minds to all of this spiritual "stuff?" What if we did not have the "eyes to see?" We all have that choice each day. Perhaps our life would not have turned out the same. By following this message, our lives have become more enriched. We have learned to follow the clues and messages each day no matter how small or large. Perhaps you might consider doing the same.

Eli Stone Got Us to Saint Anthony, Mary Magdalene, and Mother Mary

The story of Saint Anthony coming into my life has been a long journey. It took ten years to manifest fully. That, however, is how many messages come to be realized. It took a weird set of events and circumstances to manifest Saint Anthony, Mother Mary, and Mary Magdalene over those years.

It actually started while watching a TV series in 2007. There was a new pilot TV series called "Eli Stone" which looked interesting because we saw on the promos that George Michael was going to be in it. For many years after my accident I had a huge craving to play George Michael music every day since the end of 2005, which lasted to 2010.

The first pilot episode really hit a "spiritual nerve." What I mean is that something happened in that episode that was otherworldly. In the TV series, Eli Stone is a corporate attorney in a major city and happens to take unusual legal cases to help people. In this first show, a woman came in to his office to request his help in suing a corporation that makes vaccines since she believes one of their vaccines

hurt her little boy. The mom then asked Eli to come to her house to meet her child and see for himself how the child was affected. When he gets into the house and meets the child, he notices the child is playing with small square building blocks that had letters of the alphabet on them. After a while discussing things with the woman, Eli decided he should leave and as he was leaving, he noticed what the child had spelled out something with the building blocks that he had assembled. At about 13 minutes into the TV show, the child had spelled out "MAKE PEACE GEORGE MICHAEL."

Now you might not think much of that, but we did. It was because we had earlier that year got the idea of creating a small folding business-type card. The card we designed had a moon in phase representing Caroline and a star representing me and a curved line below them

representing the surface of the Earth. But inside the card, we put "MAKE PEACE." Once we saw the "Make Peace George Michael," and to see George Michael in the episode, it really felt so surreal.

Well, it does not stop with that one episode. The very next episode was titled "Freedom" and focused on a Mexican couple that the U.S. government was trying to deport. Eli won the case against the government but during the trial, the husband learned from his wife that she had a baby son in Mexico when she was very young but had to give him up. Just after the verdict, Eli and the Mexican couple were walking out of the building when they told Eli that they wanted to find that child. They asked Eli, "Where would we start to find him?" Eli, without hesitation responded "I would start at St. Anthony's Church in Roseville, California." We were stunned when we heard that because it just so happens that Roseville is the town in northern California where we live. Why didn't Eli mention some place in Mexico where she left the baby?

Why we were so shocked! Roseville was under 100,000 people at that time. We talked about this among ourselves and wondered how in the world the writers of that episode picked Roseville out of the over 400 cities in California. We checked all the church listings in Roseville for a St. Anthony. There was nothing named St. Anthony. It was so weird that I wrote a letter to the show asking how it was decided that Roseville would be included. I got no response.

Now think about it. We had two incidents in this one TV show that were so weird to us and we could not explain why all this was happening.

Two years later in 2009, we took a trip to Arizona. We had plans to go to Phoenix and then drive two hours to Flagstaff. We decided to take the old highway to Flagstaff which was a two-lane road west of Phoenix. About 45 minutes later, we happened into the small town of Wickenburg. We stopped to have breakfast. After that we walked about the town and saw in the distance a one story brick building, so we walked towards it.

As we got right up to it, we discovered it was the St. Anthony Catholic Church of Padua. We thought to ourselves where is Padua?

We tried to get inside it. But the doors were locked. Then we went to the side parking lot which also had a door but it too was locked. I pulled on it and then a person in the parking lot yelled at us. He said "If you want to get in, I can help you!" Of course, we said yes.

As he opened the door, I took three steps inside and froze. I was hit by an indescribable electrical-type energy all through my body. It was so strong I could not move my feet or body for about 15 seconds. It felt like I was holding both nodes of a car battery and I could not let go. But Caroline could not feel it. I had never experienced such powerful energy, but what was this energy? Where was it coming from? At the time there were no answers to any of our questions.

After this energy stopped, I was able to walk around in the church. All the while I was thinking what was going on in this place. We still found no answers. We then went on to Flagstaff but we were thinking about this experience that we would never forget.

Starting in 2015, Saint Anthony would be present in my psychic sessions with Kathleen along with Archangel Michael, my Dad and Mom, and others as well. I asked her why Saint Anthony is here and again there were no answers. He was just there each month when I had a session with Kathleen.

All of a sudden in one of those sessions, I got a very strong message that I had two past lives in Siracusa, Sicily. What is funny about that is that I was born about 20 miles east of Syracuse, New York, so Siracusa seemed to have a special place in my heart. Since we had done a lot of traveling to other sites around the world where we felt we had past lives, we began to plan the trip to Sicily and Siracusa.

As we were planning that trip, we thought we would start the trip in Milan and travel down Italy until we got to Sicily. We wanted to start in Milan to see "The Last Supper." As we were researching the trip and looking on the map of Italy, we saw Padua! This was the Ah-Ha! moment! So this is where Padua is! Of course we had to go to Padua on this trip. Further research revealed that the St. Anthony Basilica, the main pilgrimage site for St. Anthony is located in Padua.

When we got to Padua, we got a hotel room next to the St. Anthony Basilica. We spent several days in Padua and the surrounding area. We went inside the Basilica twice. The second time as I entered the building, I got a feeling or message to go down along the left aisle to the back. At the back was a small altar area with seats.

Then I got strong message to take a photograph of a large dark painting on the wall.

I complied and took that photograph as well as one of the larger area. It was very dark in this area and I did not see anything unusual.

The next day I was checking my iPhone and decided to look at the photographs I had taken the prior day.

As I looked, I was stunned to find the two photographs I had taken inside the Basilica. Two large beings of Light were in the photographs. How could this be happening?

We then went across town to the St. Michael Oratory built in the 1100s. It was a tiny structure and was being renovated inside. But it had ancient frescos of Archangel Michael on the wall.

We went outside the building and looked up.

Amazingly we saw a cloud with a head and face of a man and with a body! It was so clear and I took several photographs.

Was this Archangel Michael sending us his approval of coming to Padua and St. Anthony's Basilica?

When we got back to our room, I emailed those two photographs I took in the Basilica of the two Light Beings to my psychic friends back in California. I asked them what psychic information they got from them. Both responded. One said she felt both were female energy. The other said that the one in the background was Mother Mary and the other at the painting was Mary Magdalene. Caroline and I were amazed at this finding.

We had not seen anyone photograph Light Beings before and especially not Mother Mary and Mary Magdalene. Interesting to note that the Light Being in front of the painting seems to be created from the small angel in the painting.

It is no wonder that St. Anthony's Basilica is world famous and regarded as a great place of healing. Thousands of people each year go to this international shrine. It is regarded as a place of pilgrimage. Inside the Basilica is the tomb of St. Anthony which you can touch. You can feel the energy coming from it. You see, St. Anthony was a disciple of St. Francis of Assisi, and a miracle worker as well. He is known as the Saint of Lost and Stolen Articles. And as you now know, St. Anthony's Basilica is also a place of Mother Mary and Mary Magdalene.

However, this is not the end of this story. Late in 2016, Caroline and I talked about the need to reprint our last book "Simply Angelic" since we were running out of copies. However, as I sat at my computer putting all that together, I got very strong messages to do another book that combined some photographs from our three earlier books and add updated information. But then what I am going to do about a cover for this new book? The message came in strongly that those two photographs of the St. Anthony's Light Beings must be the cover. Thus this new book was born.

So you can see how we were guided for a long period of ten years from a TV show, to Wickenburg to Padua, Italy and to Saint Anthony and Mother Mary and Mary Magdalene. Needless to say, it has been quite a journey!

They Want Us to Go to Cumae

We follow messages or signs that we get all the time. It always seems to be the right thing to do. There are little messages, and then there are huge messages. This is about a huge message.

In the fall of 2012, Caroline and I went to the Napa Valley area to spend a weekend at a hot springs resort. Upon leaving that resort, we stopped in St. Helena, California. St. Helena has that small town atmosphere everyone craves. We parked downtown to find a place to have breakfast. After breakfast, we exited the building and Caroline noticed an adjacent used bookstore. In the storefront window there were books displayed. One was a coffee-table-sized book with the title "The Atlas of Mysterious Places" by Marshall Editions Limited.

Caroline immediately spotted this book and asked to go in and see the various books in the shop. I replied "We have lots of those sacred places books at home, why do we need another one?" She insisted and so we went in. A side note to mention is that Caroline often gets a feeling or message and pushes me to follow her message. So this is not unusual for us.

When we got our hands on that book, it did look interesting so we bought it. It was a reasonable price and in very good condition.

Back home the next day, I went to our local spiritual store that has crystals, readings, and so much more. As I walked in, the woman at the counter shouted at me... "Tom, you have to see this new ring... I think it is for you!" Now that was weird! But I went to the counter and looked at the ring. She was right. I could feel it was mine to have. It was a large rectangular ring with a brown background and a large black X stretching over the entire ring. She explained it was made of Andalusite. It was so unusual. It fit perfectly over my index finger and so I bought it and put it on. Upon researching it, I found that Andalusite is an ancient stone with strong protection and psychic powers.

In November as I was sitting in a chair facing the sun on a beautiful day, I decided to read that book, "Atlas of Mysterious Places" and I put it on my lap. I went page by page looking at the various sites such as Stonehenge, Machu Picchu, and Delphi. Then I got to page 48.

Immediately I felt dizzy in my chair. Then my vision started to spin and swirl. With my eyes closed, I saw a tiny X in the distance. The X started to move ever closer to me. It got bigger and bigger and then I blanked out or went unconscious. Fifteen minutes later I woke up in that chair with the book still on my lap and still turned to page 48. I felt like I had traveled somewhere as if in a dream.

I looked down and saw page 48. Page 48 was about "Cumae: Ancient Cave of Prophecy" which I had never heard of before. Upon reading the story of Cumae I found out it is on the north side of Naples, Italy. With further research, I learned it was an ancient Greek colony founded around 800 BC sitting on top of a coastal hill or cliff with views of the sea. Actually I learned that Cumae was one of many Greek settlements in southern Italy.

But Cumae was so very special because it housed the Sibyl of Cumae, a prophetess or oracle, who could predict the future. I learned that there were several Sibyls in the ancient world such as the Oracle of Delphi, and the Sibyl of Libya. The Sibyl of Cumae wrote several books that told of her prophecies. People came from far and wide to enter her cave and greet her at her throne deep in the cave and to ask her to tell them about their future.

So I determined that this Andalusite ring with the X perhaps assisted in my connection to the X in my vision sitting in that chair. Perhaps it took me magically to Cumae. There was no question now that we had to go to Cumae in Naples, Italy to follow this very strong message. What a long way to go to follow this message!

In 2013 we planned the trip to Italy with the central focus of Cumae. In September 2013, we are in Naples, Italy and we had a tour guide take us to Cumae. We find that Cumae was a large colony that is mostly destroyed now. But there are remnants of the acropolis and the Temple of Jupiter. Nearby we found the entrance to the cave of the Sibyl Cumae.

We went in the cave and noticed how well constructed the walls were and how deep it went inside the hill. I estimate the cave was 300 yards long. We finally got to the end where the Sibyl was said to be sitting on her throne. It was an awesome feeling to be in such a place of history dating back 28 centuries. We conducted some ceremonies of the spiritual kind and left a crystal to commemorate our being there.

At this point I have to back up a step to tell you what happened at a session with my psychic friend Kathleen. I had a session with her prior to going on this trip to Italy. My Dad as usual was there in the session and I could talk to him through her. His Dad came from a small town in southern Italy and emigrated to the United States about 1915. I told my Dad that I planned to go to his Dad's hometown when we arrived in Italy. My Dad responds "Don't go there, it is a waste of time. Go to Siena instead!" I said I would follow his advice and we adjusted our travel plans accordingly.

After our tour of Naples, we arrived in Siena a few days later. We still could not figure out why Dad directed us to go here. So we looked all around Siena. We were especially attracted to the Siena Cathedral built in the 1200s with its impressive architecture. So we went inside and it was so stunning that you could not believe your eyes. Then we noticed that the entire floor was made of black, white, and red marble. Not only that, the entire floor of marble was essentially a canvas of art. The marble was inlaid with images of all kinds of people, and animals that told of many stories. We were in awe when we came upon the many Sibyls etched in the marble floors of the Cathedral! All of them were large images. We wondered why? Why were they so important inside a Catholic Cathedral when in fact the Sibyls were pagan and much older than Christianity?

Our next stop was Rome, Italy and the Vatican. We had an exciting tour of the Vatican buildings and grounds. The artwork and sculptures were so impressive. When we got inside the famous Sistene Chapel, it was so crowded that we went to a corner and just tried to take it all in. All of a sudden, we noticed that there was a wide band of artwork on the lower part of the ceiling. The entire circumference of the building were paintings in the images of all the Sibyls in the world. Again, we wondered why we were seeing this. It was as though we were being guided to see the Sibyls everywhere we traveled. What would the artist Michaelangelo be thinking when he painted five Sibyls inside a Roman Catholic building? Included were the Persian, Erythraean, Delphic, Libyan, and Cumaen Sibyls as well as other prophets. There are some that suspect that the Sibyls and many aspects of Paganism were included in the evolution of Christianity. Perhaps the concept is that God accepts all people as they are all his creation.

In reflecting, this trip to Cumae was induced through a ring, a book, a vision and Dad's guidance. I have come to learn that a primary reason for Cumae for me was Soul Retrieval. It has been revealed I had several lives as a Greek in that region and I died at a young age in each of those lives. I had to retrieve my Soul Energy from those prior deaths such a long time ago in the time before Christ. Somehow the Angels above had to get me to Cumae. What better way!

Synchronicity of the Raven

In 2008, Caroline and I were going to massage appointments in a neighboring town. The masseuse was Kathleen who was at the time a new friend. She wanted to go to Egypt with us later that year but did not have all the funds. So we loaned her the $3,000 to sign up for the Egyptian Tour.

Caroline was the first to have the massage appointment that day. I spent that time just walking through the downtown area. I soon found a cute little home renovated into an art studio. What I saw through the large front window were three human-sized sculptures that got my interest. I immediately went in to see them. I was met by the artist's wife and then the artist himself. As I looked around the artist studio, there were several sculptures of Ravens. Some were very small ones that could hang on a wall and others were large ones that could only sit on a table or floor. Since Caroline was so attached to Ravens and they are her spirit guides, I felt she should come to the studio to see these while I was getting my massage.

So Caroline did just that! Later she called me to tell me to come to the studio when I was done with my massage. As I left the massage studio, Kathleen surprisingly gave me a check for $3,000 to repay us for the Egypt trip fee. This was a pleasant surprise as I certainly did not think she would repay us so soon. I was very happy to receive the money and I thought I would put that money back in the bank. Little did I know what would happen next!

As I arrived at the art studio, all four of us sat down to learn more about the artist and his wife. In the middle of the area we were sitting, there was a huge ceramic Raven sitting on a table. This Raven was heavy and large…40 inches high by 28 inches tall and 12 inches wide. It was so unique and beautiful — one of a kind.

I asked Caroline if she found something interesting to purchase, thinking that she would say she wanted that small Raven piece that was on the wall. Caroline looked at me and said "I want that big Raven on the table!" I responded "Really?" as I was surprised by her response. I asked the artist, "How much?" He said $3,300. I told Caroline that was a lot of money and where are we going to put such a huge piece of art.

After some negotiation, the artist said he would sell it for $3,000 if we bought it that day. Since Caroline was so enamored with the sculpture, I agreed to purchase it. So I told the artist we would agree to $3,000 for the piece.

The artist asked if we were sure. We said yes. His wife then asked...are you really, really sure because if you do buy it we have a story for you. We said absolutely...we want it today. Tell us the story!

Okay, the artist said, and then his wife began relating the story surrounding all of this. She began by saying that their daughter was 29 and married and could not have children so she and her husband decided to adopt a child. The adoption process was long and expensive, costing nearly $30,000. The artist said that they have helped their daughter financially to make this happen but a last payment of $3,000 was needed the very next day to complete the adoption process. She also added that they had exhausted their funds and had no more to give. He said that the adoption would not be accepted if they could not hand over that $3,000.

So the artist's wife then explained that if we bought the sculpture that day, they would have the necessary money to complete the adoption. The artist and his wife were beaming with joy since I had said "Let's get this purchase done right now."

After we left the art studio we talked about the strange set of circumstances that led to us to help someone that we did not know. We were amazed how $3,000 loaned to a friend weeks ago could be repaid unexpectedly and then be passed onto people we had just met who needed it to help their daughter adopt a baby. All in a matter of four hours. The vehicle for this was the purchase of a huge Raven sculpture which is Caroline's favorite bird and her spirit animal. It was as if we were secretly called upon to help make this adoption happen.

Well, the artist called me later to say the adoption was completed and that he, his wife, and daughter were so thankful that we and the Raven made this happen. We were so happy to help them and to have this very special Raven with a special story in our home.

Following the Guidance to Meet Emerald Alurin Stara

You might ask, "Who is this Emerald Alurin Stara?" Before 2006, I would have said the same thing. Here is the story of how she came into our lives.

In 2006, I woke up in bed in the early morning and started having a vision. Not a dream, but a vision. I started having visions in 2005 starting with the one of seeing Archangel Michael. Over the years, I have had hundreds of visions about all sorts of things.

This time, as the vision started, I saw very clearly a big rectangular object floating in mid-air. The object was thick and the top of it was a very vivid color of blue. On top of the blue, there were bright white stars. It just hovered there for the longest time and then a message spoke to me. It said "Go to Grass Valley!" And then the vision disappeared.

I told Caroline about it the next day. We talked about how we had not gone to Grass Valley for at least ten years. Grass Valley is a 45 minute drive from the Sacramento area in California. Because of our work for many years, we just never found the time to go there. It is a beautiful foothill town dating back to the Gold Rush in California. We decided to go as directed and see what could be found. We had gotten a vision to go there soon.

Two weeks later we drove up to Grass Valley. We took all afternoon and went into each downtown shop. Grass Valley has a vibrant downtown with many cute shops with unique gifts. Its old town architecture reminds one of the 1800s. But wouldn't you have guessed it, it was the last shop that gave us the answer we sought.

We came to Grass Valley at the direction of the vision. Why would the vision direct us there unless there was a reason? Well, we found The Herb Shop. It was cute and filled with clothes, gems, crystals and rocks, herbs and other things. As we looked around, I saw a sign in the back of the shop that pronounced "Tarot Card Readings with Emerald!"

Caroline and I had never had a tarot card reading so we agreed to try it. We walked back into the hallway where the tarot card reader had her office. As we entered, we met Emerald Alurin Stara, dressed in her green skirt and top and scarf. We all sat down around her table.

Then the truth started to unveil itself. She reached into her large handbag on the floor. She pulled out her deck of cards and showed them to us. I was so surprised to see her tarot cards to be identical to what I saw in my vision in design and color, even with the little white stars on top.

I told Emerald very firmly "Emerald, we were supposed to meet you today!" Then I told her of the story of my vision and being told to come to Grass Valley. We had our first of many tarot card readings with Emerald that day.

We got along so well that day. The reading was so interesting and perfect. It suggested our near term future for both of us. So since 2006, we have been coming to Grass Valley to meet her again and again for tarot readings and for her dear friendship. Probably we have seen her 25 − 30 times over the years.

We have learned a lot about ourselves from Emerald's teachings. She is very intuitive. She is also a numerologist. We had her track our past from birth to the year 2033. That was very complicated endeavor but her report showed the highlights of our past and and what might be expected in the future.

But that was not all that happened! On the way out that day, I noticed a huge number of clear crystals on a slab of rock that was so beautiful. I begged Caroline to let me buy it and she agreed. The slab of crystals was about 1 ½ feet wide by 2 ½ feet long and very heavy.

Well, wouldn't you know it, we were definitely supposed to have that slab of crystals too. Over the next few weeks as I passed it, it seemed to whisper in my head "Water me, I'm dry!" Silly to think that a crystal or a slab of hundreds of them could communicate, right?

Well, it would not stop talking to me. So in our backyard, we devised a stand with circular glass and rim where it could be watered all the time. Over the years, we could see the crystals grow. One day, the biggest crystal broke off. It was 4 inches long.

Can you believe it? We named that 4-inch crystal "Mr. Crystal" and have taken him on all our travels in the United States and around the world. He seems to have a life of his own. To finish off this story, I asked one of my psychics what she felt this Mr. Crystal was about. She responded that he wants to travel with you everywhere and then to come back home. Then he wants to be placed back on the crystal slab with all his crystal friends so he can tell his crystal friends all about the latest trip he went on with us.

When you combine this story of our Mr. Crystal and the other story later in this book with the crystal skulls Jonathan and Enoch, you have to think something is really happening with these crystals. Based on our experience with these and other crystals, we have come to believe that they have energy and even a consciousness.

The APU Send a Message

Things happen for a reason! Many times over the last few years, I would be having a vision of something and then the next morning when I am talking to Caroline, she would say, "I am just reading a book about that very thing!" It happened so many times that it could not be a coincidence. It was as if the two of us were a team working together to find answers to certain questions.

We had met some people who were putting on a tour of Peru and to places like Machu Picchu, Cuzco, the Nazca Lines, the Sacred Valley, Saksaywaman, Lake Titicaca, and so much more. The tour was to begin in early November 2007. Both of us were very excited about the trip.

When we decide to go on a trip outside the country, we like to do a lot of research of that country and any sacred or special sites that we would like to visit. So Caroline bought several books on Peru. One of them told about the legends of the Inca who inhabited Peru for a long period of time.

One night about two months before the trip was to begin, I was wakened to view a very strong vision. It was like a little movie. It began with me in what appeared to be an ancient Catholic Church or Cathedral. I was inside the large main lobby and standing to the right of me is what looks like a Catholic Bishop dressed so formally in his attire. The Bishop then points to the left to indicate he wanted me to see who is coming through the main arched entry into the Cathedral.

In my vision, I am thinking this cannot be happening. I can see three very tall beings which appeared to be about fifteen feet tall. Incredibly, these three beings were not walking into the Cathedral...they were floating into it. They appeared to have human-like features but were draped in full white hooded robes.

The next thing I see is that these three beings were floating over to me. They all looked at me as they passed by. But the one in the middle stopped right in front of me and bent completely over to look me right in the face. It seemed his face was about three feet in distance from my face. Then they floated away and the vision was completed. I thought that this vision was so unique but I could not figure it out.

It did not take long to get the answer. The next morning at breakfast, I told Caroline about the vision I had last night and described these three beings. She sat back in her chair with the book she was reading and said quite firmly, "You just described in detail the APU!" I said, "Who are the APU?"

I was amazed that she had the answer. How could she know? She went on to describe that the book she was reading was about the legends of the Inca. She said the Inca believed that 65 million years ago, beings from another planet came to Earth and seeded or created all the life, including us. She went on to say that the white robes are characteristic, and that they float over the ground even though they have legs and feet. She explained that the APU float because they do not want to contaminate the Earth in any way. She said the APU look after us as if we are their children in a way and are concerned with the health of the planet.

I guess in a way we were being prepared for our trip to Peru. About a month before we left for Peru, I had a session with my psychic friend Linda Schooler. I wanted to see if she was picking up any information for me for the trip.

Linda said that my spirit guides wanted me to be sure to see how the ancient Inca buildings were constructed without any mortar and that everything precisely fit like a puzzle. When we got to Cuzco and Saksaywaman high in the Andes Mountains, you could easily see such buildings. In some cases, the bricks or blocks were precisely cut as if with a modern laser and put together without any mortar. In Saksaywaman, the walls were built of 50 to 100 ton boulders that fit so perfectly together and on top of each other.

Now you have to wonder how this ancient civilization could cut blocks so precisely, and how they could stack such heavy boulders on top of each other. Either the Inca had much more advanced technology or powers than our current civilization, or they had help from others. Some speculate that these powers or help possibly came from Alien Beings from another planet or dimension.

In my opinion, the message from the APU to me was that they were real. Having the vision, learning about the APU, and seeing first hand the ancient architecture of the Inca changed our lives and perspective on our world and its history.

Perhaps there was a race of APU that helped create the life on Earth and that they are still so very interested in us and how we are doing. So interesting to think about, isn't it?

The trip to Peru seemed to be a launching point for future trips and learning so much more about our planet and its history. It was also the start of my interest in clouds and how they can send messages to us. You see, on the train from Cuzco to Machu Picchu, I noticed some funny clouds through the ceiling window of the train car. I saw this huge cloud in the form of a bird, and then a large cat cloud next to it. Later in the trip I saw a large snake over the town of Puna on the shores of Lake Titicaca. I did not know it at the time, but I was later to figure out that I was shown the three Inca Gods of the Condor, the Puma, and the Snake...but in cloud form. From that moment on until today, I have to always look at the clouds to see what they might show me.

An Angel Came to Visit Me at the Supermarket

In 2015, I had an Angel show up during a car accident. Usually you hear about how the Angel saved your life in a terrible car accident. But not this time!

That day I went grocery shopping at our local supermarket. I parked in the perpendicular aligned parking spaces where you have to back out into the traffic lane. I have parked there for years each time I go to the market.

This time, even though I was careful in backing into the lane, something bad happened — or was it? As I was slowly backing out, I could hear a loud crunch. I got out of my red Chevy Tahoe SUV, and I saw that I had backed into a Cadillac car that was turning into a parking space next to mine.

The damage to the Cadillac was horrendous. I could not believe that just backing out at a 1 mile per hour speed would cause the other driver's door to be so smashed in. I got out and met the driver, a woman who was upset of course. She said I caused the accident. I could not believe I caused it because I checked in all directions before backing out. But I could not refute that I did back into her.

We exchanged driver information. She explained that she just got into an accident with another car the prior week. And that this Cadillac was a rental until the other is fixed. We surveyed her damage and then I looked at the rear of my Chevy Tahoe. There was no damage! The right rear bumper of my Chevy Tahoe is what hit her Cadillac. As I inspected that area more, what appeared was an image imprinted on the bumper — an Angel image with wings in white so perfect that it looked like an artist designed it and stuck it right there. I could not believe it and took pictures. What was most astounding and significant to ponder was it was a perfect Angel-like image. There were no other marks on the bumper, not even a tiny scratch. Impossible!

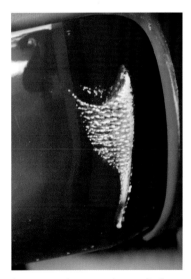

Interestingly, the woman and I started to have a nice conversation about our lives and I ended up giving her a copy of our last book "Simply Angelic – Divine Images." What appeared to be a bad thing, turned out to be a very nice experience.

For some reason, I believe an Angel wanted me to meet that woman and give her a copy of our book. Who can figure why things happen the way they do? There always appears to be a reason if you search for it. Nonetheless, two years later I smile every time I approach my Chevy Tahoe I still see that white Angel image and knowing that there was a reason for that accident.

The Meeting of the Crystal Skulls, Jonathan and Enoch

Our friend Kathleen is a therapeutic healing intuitive. Several years ago, I was getting a session from her and she got a "message" in her mind from her crystal skull that he wanted to meet my crystal skull Enoch. I asked how this is possible?

The story actually began when I fell in love with a clear crystal skull when I was led to meet an older woman in the Palm Springs area. Her name was Mary and she invited Caroline and I to her small home. There I spotted this beautiful crystal skull which was about the size of a hand. I asked Mary if I could buy it from her. Mary said it is too special to her to part with it. When Mary died about three years later, I was stunned to receive an unexpected package in the mail. Mary had the crystal skull sent to us just before she died...it was that special crystal skull she named Enoch. What a wonderful surprise for me! Meet Enoch and Jonathan below....

About the same time, Kathleen had purchased her crystal skull in northern California. It was about the same size as Enoch but it was more of a lavender color. Kathleen said she was in a shop and it called out to her to buy it. The skull told her his name was Jonathan. Kathleen is attuned to messages coming into her mind and she follows the directions, just as I do. She later told me that Jonathan said to her that he wanted to meet Enoch.

A few days later, I brought Enoch over to Kathleen's home and we set both crystal skulls about 6 inches apart on top of a cabinet in one of Kathleen's extra bedrooms. The cabinet was about chest high. Almost immediately as Kathleen and I watched the two skulls, the room's door slammed shut! So hard it created a slight breeze and almost hit us. We both looked at each other in amazement. We said to each other at the same time "That was so powerful!" "How could this happen?" Amazed, we left the room and closed the door so that Jonathan and Enoch could have some privacy. Obviously, they had a lot to talk about and share.

While crystal skulls are rumored to be powerful, could they be this powerful to make a door slam shut? It is also said that crystal skulls are conscious beings and can communicate with other crystals and with people. Clearly, this incident was proof to us that it was true. Think about it next time you walk past a crystal skull or any crystal for that matter! Are there more forms of life here on Earth than we have been taught or could even imagine? I definitely think so.

The Magic of the Number 11

After he passed, my Dad started to talk to me through Kathleen during a psychic session. The first thing he said was "Son, when you get here you will realize that it is all about numbers!"

I have always been enamored with the number 11. I was born on 11-11 and as I evolved spiritually, I researched and found that 11 is a very spiritual number. Many people have told me that they have been seeing the numbers 11, 111 and 1111 and wonder why. I have been having that experience for many decades now.

According to experts in spirituality, seeing the number 11 is a sign that you are connected with angels, archangels, or your personal guides. In a way, it is a message from them that they are here with you at that moment. Perhaps it is just to comfort you, or to guide you to information, or send you a message that is important for you to recognize at that time.

I have seen 11, 111 or 1111 all through my life and did wonder why but just assumed it was connected to my birth date or a coincidence. After my terrible vehicle accident in 2001, seeing 11s became more pronounced and seemed to guide me to certain messages I was receiving. In fact, when I analyzed my accident, I realized that it was 11:11. The accident was on Highway 65 so 6 plus 5 equals 11. The accident happened on February 9, again 2 plus 9 equals 11. I began to recognize that seeing 11s was a way to awaken us to the spiritual side of things.

I agree with my Dad that it is all about numbers here also. There is a significance to numbers which we often take for granted. Our civilizations run on numbers in so many ways.

Let me tell you of some instances where I saw it play out for me. First, my wife Caroline is aligned to me by the number 11.

I was sixteen the year I came to California with my parents in 1965. My parents bought a house on a street where I did not know anyone. Near the end of that first year, I was driving my Dad's car down our street and then I saw this beautiful girl in her front yard watering the yard. I wanted to stop but I was too shy to even try. I waved and drove by.

That week I would drive down that street several times and amazingly she was always there in her front yard and each time I would wave at her. Being shy, I just could not get the courage to stop.

The final time I drove down that street, I think I got my first psychic or spiritual message ever. I was perhaps 150 feet from that girl but I could see her in her yard. Then all of a sudden, I got a whisper of a message in my left ear from a female voice which declared "You have to stop!" While I was surprised at that message, I thought to myself, "What is the worst that could happen if I asked her out...she could just say no!" So I did stop and talked to her and asked her out and she said "YES!"

Caroline was two years younger than myself and just about to start her junior year in high school. I had just graduated. We continued to date that summer and then I was off to a nearby state college that fall. I was thinking to myself that I would also date college girls as well. Boy, was I so wrong!

I asked and asked for dates in college. And I always got rejected. At least ten attempts and that certainly made me self-conscious about dating. So each week I would call Caroline and ask her for a date. She would always be there for me.

The second year of our dating we decided to get serious and plan our marriage. We decided to wait until after I graduated from college in two years. That is exactly what happened. We were married on 8/29. The 29 again equals 11. Of course we had many discussions about how we came to be together and why we picked that day for our wedding.

I learned that Caroline was born on October 1. Why am I telling you this? Because she is an 11. Add October [the tenth month plus 1 for her date of birth] and you get 11. There is no doubt in our minds that our coming together was planned through the use of numbers. Most likely the angels above had a heavy hand in this reunion. Not only did that female voice guide me to stop at Caroline's house, but also likely prevented me from getting any other dates in college so that I would always return to Caroline.

One day we were discussing how we got together, all the number 11 "coincidences," and how I ended up living on her street that she had lived on since 1957. So we walked down our street and counted the number of houses on the same side of the street. You guessed it. There were 11 houses including hers and mine! That just about sealed it for us. Perhaps there was a purpose in us getting together and becoming life partners.

As of this writing, we have been married for about 47 years and been together for 50 years. It is clear to us that we were guided to be together all these years. After further recent research of our Past Lives [we do believe in reincarnation], we have found that we have been together during several lives in our past in Ireland and Italy. I guess you would call our lives today as a reunion.

The number 11 continues to play out with my parents as well. They both died in 2011. My Dad passed at the age of 92, which is an 11 when added together, and my Mom passed at the age of 83, again an 11.

Whenever we see the numbers 11,111, or 1111 or combinations that equate to 11, we know that we are getting a message about what we doing at that time.

Some people may pass these occurrences as just coincidence. But given these instances and so many more I have not shared, there is no doubt in our minds that numbers drive the events in our lives. If Dad is correct that the afterlife is all about numbers, why wouldn't the same be true on Earth?

Perhaps you might think about the numbers in your life. You might even consider having a session with a numerologist to see how numbers play out for you.

1111

The Magic of Eleven

The Magic Energy of December 21, 2012

During the month of December 2012, the airwaves were filled with talk of the end of the world. There was even a movie entitled "2012" which was released about that time. It was a fictional account of how the world would tragically end on 12-21-12. People were predicting Doomsday!

It was my understanding that most of this talk came from the ancient Mayan civilization's Long-Count Calendar. Apparently the idea was that the end of the world would coincide with the end of their 5,126-year-long calendar cycle. That end of the cycle was about December 2012. Many people really believed that the world would end on that date. The hysteria was fueled by the media, movies, and general conversation among people.

Caroline and I had a very tough time in 2011 and 2012. We had seen my Mom and Dad pass and also Caroline's Dad and Aunt pass as well. We felt it was time to take a break and try to heal and re-energize ourselves. So we planned a trip to Oahu, Hawaii. We wanted to have a quiet Christmas together. For whatever reason, we planned the trip for the week of December 21, 2012. We did not realize we would be traveling on December 21st.

We arrived at our hotel in Waikiki in the morning of December 21st. We felt that Hawaii would be a great way to get some sun, relax, and tour the island. We had been to Hawaii many times over the years and nothing seemed abnormal about our trip.

That very day we walked the beaches, had dinner, and just enjoyed the whole environment. That night we went to bed without any hint of what was to come the next day.

On December 22nd, we got up early and had breakfast, then walked for a couple of hours and just took in the scenery and the sun. By noon, we were so exhausted so we went back to our room. We discussed with each other how tired we felt and how this was not normal for us. Usually we could go all day and not be tired. We decided to rest in the room and take a nap. Our nap became several hours long. When we woke up we were still very tired and we decided to stay in the room the rest of the night. This was turning out to be a different kind of trip for us. We normally would make plans to go out each night for dinner and drinks and music. We had planned to rent a car and tour the island.

On December 23rd, the same thing happened to us. We felt good in the morning and had breakfast and walked a bit, but by noon, we were so tired we had to go back to the room for the rest of the day and night. This pattern was repeated each of the seven days we were in Hawaii. We just could not figure out what was happening to us. This was very unusual for us. We typically have so much energy to do whatever we want, especially on wonderful trips like this.

I felt particularly different. I no longer wanted to have any alcoholic drinks, or wine. I was not one to overuse alcohol, but I normally would want a glass or two of wine. Not anymore! In fact, alcohol in any form now was revulsive to me. I did not miss it at all. Caroline also told me that she also had the same feeling, but not as severe.

So we spent the week in Hawaii mostly in our room or resting in the lounge chairs next to the pool. Imagine spending all the money for the air flight and hotel and all you do is spend 20 hours a day in your room. Just laying around was not what we expected.

When we arrived back home, it seemed at first that nothing had changed. Soon we decided to go to one of our favorite restaurants and bar in Auburn, California, located in the foothills. We had to separate first for an appointment, so I arrived at the restaurant first. I took three steps inside it and I stopped. It felt like a bouncer was at the entrance and he put his hands on my chest to prevent me from going any further. I noticed I felt nauseous and it felt like that place was full of evil and negative energy. I quickly walked out. Later I saw Caroline nearby. She said she went in without me also and came out with the same exact feeling that the place was so very negative now. We wondered how such a great place now felt so terrible for us. What had happened?

This pattern repeated itself in regard to each of our favorite places to dine and drink. Time after time we felt that negative energy. We had to leave each place immediately. What was happening? It got to be that we had to stay home most of the time. There were just not any places that we now felt comfortable.

It did not stop there! Eventually, we both felt repelled by anything negative or that had negative energy. We became so much aware of anything around us that was negative, and we had to eliminate it from ourselves and our environment. All the negativity on TV was now not acceptable for us to watch. It also included places, people we might encounter, and family and friends. The result was that now we were living a life of positivity. All we knew was that on that day of December 21st, everything changed for us. What happened to cause that?

Well, there were reports that very special energies from outer space were coming into our planet on that very day. The Earth gets bombarded with different energies each day. However, these energies were different and we think they changed us. Perhaps this is what the Mayan calendar was predicting. Since December 2012 was the end of the 5,126 Long Count Calendar, it symbolized the end of a cycle and the beginning of another cycle. In other words, the death of one cycle and the rebirth of another. Perhaps it was based on special energies coming into the Earth due to the alignment of planets, stars, and what is the called the Central Sun – the center of our galaxy.

It is now 2017 and the changes to our bodies and our life remain as they started that trip to Hawaii in December 21st 2012. Perhaps it is weird to think that something could change us both in one night without us knowing! But to us, there is no question about it. Those energies changed our bodies and our minds. In a way, it was a rebirth for each of us.

Frankly, you have to call it MAGIC! We are so much happier now with these changes. Our lives are filled with positivity. We have removed all the negative influences in our lives on a daily basis. If someone comes to us with negativity, we walk away. If we go into places that have negative energies, we leave. If a TV channel shows us negative things, we change the channel to beautiful music. Looking back, we could have fought this. In other words, we could have walked into those negative restaurants and stayed. Or continued to be around negative people. But what would have been the result? It seems a law of nature is that negativity breeds more negativity, and positive breeds more positive. It is all about CHOICE! We are so glad we chose a positive life. Actually, I believe everyone can choose a life of the positive. With a bit of courage, decisiveness, and persistence, it can be accomplished.

Perhaps you might want to think about how you could change your life to be more positive.

Rise to the Power of Positivity

The Water Leaks Kept On and On

My parents bought a new home in 1980. One month later, they were so shocked to find their house was flooded with water when they came home after going to the grocery store. The copper pipe had busted near the water heater that was located in the hallway.

Years later, the water leaks continued. In 2010, my parents were becoming severely ill and we had to relocate them to a local Senior Care Facility. Now Caroline and I had to care for their home too.

Soon, when I would go to check their house, I would find leaks in the landscape irrigation system. Over a period of two years, there were about 30 leaks in different locations of the system. One day, I fixed a leak in the plastic pipe that was near the outside wall of the house. I walked away, and then a huge spray of water rose into the air. Another leak, this time near the last leak I just had repaired! I fixed that one and then I walked out of the side yard area and I hear another leak in the same general location. Now, I am wondering what the heck is going on!

A total of five leaks occurred that hour on that day at that same location. It seemed impossible. Then I went to check my parents' large backyard pool. The skimmer device that circulates within the water to pick up debris was doing fine. Then it moved towards me like a snake and all of a sudden, the back flexible hose that propels the skimmer raised out of the water and squirted a large quantity of water right on my groin area. Now that was unbelievable! I thought to myself it seems that the skimmer was alive and knew what it was doing. Was it foolish to think that? Or was the skimmer yelling for help?

Just for fun, I called our friend Jaap van Etten who had helped us out so much with negative entities or energies attached to Caroline and myself. I asked him to scan my parent's property and house. I didn't expect him to say what he did. Unbelievably, Jaap said that there was a WATER BEING under the slab of the house. He found this out by contacting a benevolent Djinn being who told him that the Water Being was left there by the Maidu Native Americans who lived in the area roughly 150 to 200 years ago. The Djinn went on to explain that the Maidu held ceremonies in the nearby creek area and conjured up the Water Being, but they never released it. So the Water Being was stuck underground when the house slab was poured in 1980. The Djinn advised Jaap that to release the Water Being it would be necessary to drill a hole through the concrete slab deep enough to reach the soil or to mentally move the Water Being to the open side yard and release it. Jaap thanked the Djinn. He then mentally moved the Water Being to the side yard so it could be released to go back to the creek area. Sounds crazy doesn't it?

Yet, we wondered if that would work. There have not been any minor or major water problems on the property for several years now. Caroline and I have so much gratitude to Jaap and his amazing talents.

We Are Supposed to Have "Free Will"

One of the things that makes each of our lives special is that we can exercise Free Will. We can choose what we wish to do each day. Other people may try to influence us, persuade us, or even force us to do something, but ultimately, each of us can make our own decisions. Think about all the decisions we make each day. When to get up, what to have for breakfast, how we approach work that day, how we take care of our families, who we chose to meet with and what we will say to them, and the list goes on. Perhaps we take for granted these freedoms.

During the period of 2005 through 2009, I was excited and at the same time frustrated with the spiritual events occurring all around me and inside me. At one point, I actually felt like I had another person inside me. I know it sounds weird and unbelievable. Through my investigations and readings, I discovered it was true. I had fourteen dead ancestral spirits and the Djinn attached to my body. This was verified by the person I consulted. He is Jaap van Etten, a trained professional who specializes in identifying entities attached to you and how to remove them. In addition, during this period, I would often wake up to find red markings on my body...arms, legs, and back. The question in my mind was if I was under attack. How do I fight this? Will I survive it?

In 2009, I went to see my wonderful psychic Francie Marie. We talked a bit about all this and then I asked her "What if I just went back to living like a normal person instead of following all this spiritual stuff?" Francie Marie is very talented in reaching your angels and guides. A short time later, she said "Tom, they are saying imagine a dam with a big reservoir behind it. And then the dam breaks and the force of the water in the reservoir is so huge it destroys everything in its path." She added that they are saying "This will happen to you Tom, if you change." I said to her "Wait a minute – what about Free Will?" "I thought everyone has Free Will?" She responded by saying they said you don't have Free Will anymore.

That was such a meaningful answer to me. Francie Marie had given me so much accurate information in the past including predictions that she made about what will happen that all came true. So I had to believe what she just said to me.

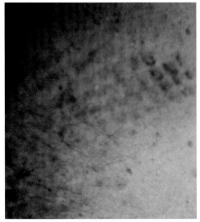

With that in mind, I said "Okay, I won't fight it anymore!" I told her I will be patient and continue following guidance. Later in 2009, I went back to her to show her the latest red mark on my body. It was the largest one ever. It was huge, the size of a person's hand and on my right shoulder blade. It was so red but there was no pain. This red mark appeared overnight and lasted for five days and then disappeared just as mysteriously.

So I showed Francie Marie a photograph of this red mark. Quite quickly she responded saying that they want you to know you completed your Initiation. But Initiation for what?

Can you imagine if I had gone to the doctor and showed him or her my red marks each time they happened? What would have been the treatment? Would he or she have recommended a psychological analysis or some drug to supposedly remove the marks?

So now it made more sense to me what I was going through all those years. In retrospect, I was right not to fight it but to go with the flow of all the guidance and messages I would receive each day. So many remarkable things have happened since 2009. I would have missed all those opportunities if I had fought my path or ignored all the messages. I am convinced that these red marks were a part of the process of spiritual evolution in my case.

Many people experience what I have experienced and wonder what is happening to them. Perhaps my experiences offer some help to them. Again, the words "Breathe, Believe, and Receive" are so meaningful.

Love and Peace

Linda Schooler Predicts That I Will Paint

I love art. We have collected artwork in our travels to many places around the world including Australia, Ireland, England, France, Italy, Hawaii, Canada, and the Caribbean. But I never thought I could create a decent piece of art through painting it myself. All I remember is that I could do those finger paints in kindergarten!

This story is about painting. It started with me meeting Linda Schooler for a psychic session in October 2007. One of the amazing things she said was that I would paint shortly after we return from our trip to Peru in early November. I told her "Linda you are crazy...I cannot paint!"

She went on to emphatically say that I would paint. She said her guides were saying for me not to worry what it looks like...just paint. I told Linda "This is impossible. I don't paint and I am too busy anyway to paint!" Then she said something I have never forgotten. She said **"Tom, the energy is so strong saying you will paint, I believe it will happen for you!"** I have never heard of a psychic emphasize a prediction so strongly. She was very convinced. I was still very skeptical.

We went to Peru and got back in mid-November. After a few days, we went to the nearby foothill town of Auburn, California. It was a beautiful day...a clear sunny sky and warm. Caroline had an appointment so I entertained myself by walking the downtown area. Suddenly, in mid-step, some electrical type energy hit me on top of my head, then traveled down my head into my throat and landed in my stomach. The best way I can describe this energy is to tell you that it felt like touching your car battery and feeling the energy given off by that. Yes, it was very strong.

Instantly, I got a message from my stomach area and that energy. Can you believe that? The message was one word...PAINT! In a sense, this is hard to describe. You had to be there! The message was compelling, addictive, and demanding. There was no doubt. I could not resist it. I had to follow the message. How could this be happening? Just unbelievable!

So when I met back up with Caroline, I had to tell her what just happened to me and that we had to go to the art store right away. She was a bit stunned but she had learned to trust me based on all the incidents that had already happened since 2001. So we went to our local art store and I bought canvases, paint, brushes. I did not really know what I was doing.

The energy was so strong that I had to start painting immediately after dinner that night. I painted for several hours. And then the next night, and the next, for several days. The addiction to paint was within me and I could not resist it.

What I could not believe was that my first painting was so good. It was of a Lion! You must understand that I was not painting a Lion at all, but I felt like my hand was being guided and the

result was the Lion. What was funny was that the Lion was my favorite animal. I don't know why, but all my life I have been drawn to the Lion. You might call it my Spirit Animal. The draw of the Lion makes me watch just about any show on TV that has a lion in a movie or show. To this day, I cannot stop watching that movie "Gladiator."

So I have continued to paint for years now. I have shown my art in local galleries, and in restaurants and cafes. I paint because I must paint. As part of the painting exercise, I find at times, my hand is moving on its own to create something. Or I get a message to use a certain color or design. It feels like the Angels are guiding me.

Many people say my paintings really "speak" to them. Others say they feel the energy coming from them. I cannot explain it all, so I just go with the flow and paint when it feels right to do so.

They say that music and art are the language of the Angels. I believe that to be true. Perhaps the Angels are talking to me or through me and I can pass on their message to others through the art work. See some of my other paintings to the side.

Nevertheless, what a remarkable experience to have felt this electrical type energy come through my head to my stomach and compel me to paint. All I can say is that it is MAGIC! It has changed my life and made me a more creative person.

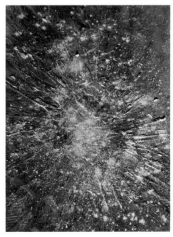

The Spiritual Journey Is Not All a Bed of Roses!

In 2001, Archangel Michael spoke to me in my Jeep to give me directions on how to save my life during the accident that was to come. After that, my world started to change in so many ways.

About two months later, a strange woman came up to me and told me I must journal each day because my life was going to change. How did she know? Without hesitation, she just walked away. In retrospect, that woman was likely an Angel in human form giving me this important message. I have had several such messages by strangers over the years.

The message was so strong that I started journaling immediately. Sixteen years later, her message was so right. I would have forgotten so many things that have happened to me if I had not done the journaling.

I then met a man in 2003 during my search for what was happening to me. He was an astrologer and very intuitive. The first thing he said was "By 2008, you will have divorced your wife or your marriage will never be the same again." That sounded so impossible. Caroline and I were very happy in our marriage and had been together 33 years at that time. How could he say this? Frankly, I had already met so many women in the spiritual trades and I was amazed at how many were divorced. The common thread was that their husband did not understand or accept that something spiritual was happening to his wife. Was this our fate?

In 2004, something weird and terrible began to happen around me. Nearly every time I was close to Caroline, I would see and feel a spirit. It was a terrible negative spirit or energy. This happened so frequently, I did not know what to do. I got the sense from that spirit that it wanted to hurt or kill me, and if it could not do that, it wanted to destroy our marriage. The spirit got so close to me I could see its face, touch it, and feel its skin so to speak. I could actually feel its Evil! I got to thinking that this astrologer was right.

I communicated this to Caroline. But she did not see or feel anything about this spirit. Imagine you are seeing something nobody else sees. How are you to prove it exists? Will people think you are crazy or just seeing things? This evil spirit was with me month after month until late 2005. As a result, I was so frustrated, depressed and angry. I felt helpless!

In December 2005, I was at wits end. Suddenly one day, I started to get this craving to play and hear George Michael music constantly. George was the musician from Britain who started out with the group WHAM! and then went solo. This feeling was so strong I had to play his music while going to work and coming home. I had to play it while at home. Over and over I would play it either on the radio, or the many George Michael CDs I had purchased. Why was I doing this?

I went to a couple of psychics on this issue. They said that Archangel Michael was telling me through the music that he was there with me and protecting me from this Evil around me. This craving lasted into 2010 and then it stopped. Imagine five years of playing this music!

One day in 2007, Caroline and I decided to go to the nearby café for lunch. As we went in, we noticed a male friend of ours. We went over to greet him. He was with a woman who we had never met. He introduced her and said she was from Flagstaff, Arizona. He asked how I was doing and I told him of this evil presence in my life. All of a sudden, this woman says to call a man she knows who lives near Sedona, Arizona. She said to call Jaap van Etten and he should be able to help me with this evil spirit. Well, I did call him and he said he can remotely remove such spirits from my body and my home. Thankfully, this man was successful in removing that evil spirit. Jaap became a vital resource to me as this evil spirit was one of many to come and attach to my body and Caroline's body. You never know when you might get help from a stranger who guides you to another person that can solve your problem. Were the angels at work in this case?

But the battle was still raging within me. This was because I still felt like I was living with another person inside me. It was true that another energy entered my body. The questions were "who was this" and "why me?" I called Jaap again and he scanned Caroline and myself. After the scan, he determined that we each had 14 ancestral spirits and at least one Djinn attached to our bodies.

He said the ancestral spirits are remnants of the Native American Tribe that inhabited our area many years ago. Often, the Djinn are very powerful beings that just do not like human beings. One of the stories I have read about the Djinn is that they were a creation of God before human beings. When God created us, the Djinn were angry and did not want to acknowledge us even though God asked them to honor his new creation...us. In other words, the Djinn have never gotten over the fact that God created us. The Djinn can see us but we cannot see them.

Again, Jaap was successful in removing them from our bodies. But all this was taking a toll on our minds and our bodies. Caroline was becoming more of a believer in what was happening to me because now it was happening to her.

One day in 2010, Caroline and I were at my parents' Senior Care Facility to meet them for lunch. My mom was terrified as she told me that I have to be careful as someone was trying to assassinate me that very day. Indeed, to hear this from my mom was quite startling and very important to me. She was the type of person who was so level-headed and not emotional. Her care provider said this was all she could talk about all morning. The caregiver also said that her sister is a psychic and that her sister had called her in the morning to tell her that someone was going to kill me. That was so strange to hear since I didn't even know her sister or had even contacted her in any way. I ended up talking to the sister and she detailed the information that she was receiving about me and for me to be very careful. It all seemed so surreal and I still had my doubts.

Caroline and I went home. Later that afternoon with all this on our minds, I was looking out of our kitchen window and spotted a strange car parked across the street. I could see the occupants as the car was facing our house. I got my camera with the zoom lens so I could see the German Shepherd dog standing up in the passenger seat and a man was covering his face with a newspaper. I got the sense that the dog was very smart and perhaps was in charge. It all felt so evil. So I took some photographs of them and immediately downloaded them on my computer. Perhaps the notion that I would be killed that day was right because those photographs show so many tiny black evil-looking little creatures filling the inside of the car. My eyes could not see them, but the camera could.

About 15 minutes later, I went out to the kitchen and I could see that the car was still there. So maybe I was a little rash, but I had enough. I went out to confront this man. As soon as I got halfway there, he immediately dropped his newspaper and drove off rapidly. Maybe there was something to this idea of someone trying to hurt me!

In 2013, we were preparing to publish our third book "Simply Angelic." We had to drive to the San Francisco Bay Area to meet Lorna, our book shepherd, to finalize the draft book. We had a great final meeting and left knowing the book would now get published and printed. After the meeting, Caroline and I decided to drive to the Pacific Coast and stay overnight at the ocean somewhere. However, as we were driving on the outskirts of town, all of a sudden, my sunglasses rapidly flew off my face towards the steering column. In mid-air, they broke in half like someone was using their hands to do that! Just before they left my face, I felt a force that brushed against my left ear. Since all the windows were closed on the car, the only explanation was that some entity was at work against us. At the same moment, the dash on our car lit up. The icon that was lit was a symbol of a tire with a diagonal line through it. We pulled over to the side of the road to try to figure this all out. We got out the manual and that icon meant that if you see it, it means your wheels were spinning. It seemed to us that the spirit in our car was telling us that somehow our book was not going to be published. I felt it was trying to scare us.

This incident was further proof to us that evil was around us and we had to get rid of it. So I called Jaap again and he was successful in getting rid of the entity...again another Djinn.

However, the evil persisted. It seemed that there was no end to the evil trying to invade our bodies and our home. One day in 2015, a long-haired black cat came into our backyard. It was injured and likely was seeking help. It had two large holes on the top of its lower back. They were bleeding and had a lot of pus. Our feeling was that the cat had been attacked by a dog, snake, or even a hawk. We fed the cat and cleaned up the wounds. We felt that we should help the cat for several days before we took it to the veterinarian. A few days later the cat was walking in our backyard and I noticed a funny-looking image on the hind section of the left leg. I took some photographs of it and when I looked at them, it showed up as a humanoid figure and it looked like something evil. It was so weird, I emailed Jaap with that photograph and he told me that indeed it was an evil entity. He said that the evil entity was using the cat as a way to get into our home and us as it knew we would care for the cat. Again, Jaap came to our rescue and removed the entity from the cat and our home. Within a week, the cat's scraggly fur was healed into a shiny beautiful coat. We call him "Black."

These are a few examples of the types of things we were experiencing which put so much stress on Caroline and myself. I did some thinking about it all and a thought came to mind. What I am living seems so similar to the journey of the salmon home to lay its eggs. The salmon has to journey hundreds of miles upstream. It has to face obstacles along the way such as river rapids, predators like the bear, fishermen and poachers trying to catch them, even river pollution. It is a long and scary journey for them.

I am often amused when I think about our existence on Earth. Perhaps in a way, Earth is the "Pain Planet!" If you think about our everyday existence, each day we probably have a pain somewhere in our body. It could be slight or very painful. We could be hurting because of an injury, or a birth ailment, or disease. We could be addicted to illegal or legal drugs, food, or alcohol. We could be hurting emotionally through a bad relationship, or someone making fun or bullying us. We could be depressed emotionally as well. There are so many ways we can feel pain or experience the difficulties of life each and every day. So perhaps our struggle here on Earth is to test us. To test our ability to survive all that is put before us. To test our courage and our mental/intuitive abilities to figure out solutions. Caroline and I have had our share of physical pain and suffering within our bodies. In addition, we have had to deal with the suffering accompanied with persistent Evil energies trying to control us.

Fortunately, as human beings, most of us have the capacity to find the solutions to alleviate or reduce the pain within our bodies. We even have the ability to seek out skilled people who can remove Evil from our bodies or our spaces, as we did through the help of Jaap van Etten. Perhaps this is the test of our abilities to find solutions on Earth that are all around if you look for them.

I think the journey many people have to endure on their own spiritual path might be quite similar to the Salmon or concept of the "Pain Planet." It certainly has been for us. You have to have the will to endure. You have to have patience and persistence. You cannot be discouraged to the point of quitting. You have to have that deep hunger to continue each day no matter what happens to you. Yes, there are many great and wonderful things that happen as well. The person that is on his or her spiritual path must have that supreme will and motivation to survive all that confronts them in order to be successful and to find what finally awaits them.

Along the way, one learns so many lessons. Our experiences have taught us that the most important lesson is that you must have Love in your Heart and Mind. In fact, the remedy for all those evil spirits is to hold yourself in a state of Love at all times. Love is the shield and protection against all those who wish to harm you whether it is another person or an Evil entity. Who would have thought that Love would be so important!

Abundance

Chapter 3

The Afterlife is Not the End

Don't be satisfied with the stories that come before you,
unfold your own myth.

— Rumi

Not I – nor anyone else – can travel that road for you.
You must travel it yourself.

— Walt Whitman

Reincarnation and the Imperminence of Clouds

By Reverend Judith M. McLean, PhD

In our authors' fourth volume on clouds, Tom and Caroline Lumbrazo are sharing some of their past life experiences. They asked me to clarify, examine, and explain the concept of reincarnation, rebirth, re-embodiment or transmigration of the soul. In my own spiritual journey, I originally believed in a literal and very sequential concept of reincarnation, like most followers of the theory of rebirth. However, after thirty-seven years of deep meditation, I have come to perceive the idea of the soul moving from lifetime to lifetime as more complicated than one might think. I believe there are many aspects of past lives that are possible.

The belief in reincarnation has been around in Asian cultures for thousands of years. Buddhists and Hindus are the predominant religions that contain such an acceptance of rebirth. However, it is not only eastern cultures that have this thought system. The early Greeks, Romans, Celts, and Cathars of France did as well. Little known is that the Native Americans of the Pacific Northwest and the Inuits of Alaska and Canada also had after-death views of being reborn. Additionally, some of the Middle Eastern religions have entertained the thought or believed the possibility. References to John the Baptist and Elijah in several of the gospels (Mark, Luke, and John, and the Old Testament book of Malachi) seem to equate John the Baptist with the reincarnation of Elijah the ascended prophet. However, this is contested by Orthodox Christianity. But reincarnation was a belief system in many of the early Christian sects before the Council of Nicaea in 325 AD. This first council with Christian bishops and the Roman Emperor Constantine met to settle many early Christian disputes of theology and belief. The Council made a determination to eliminate many of the existing Christian gospels and the concept of reincarnation. The other gospels and theologies of early Christianity were deemed heretical and suppressed. It has only been since the latter part of the 20th century that these alternative gospels have been found as with the Nag Hammadi Manuscripts, the Dead Sea Scrolls, and other findings of early gospels.

Reincarnation contains many possibilities. Our soul can decide to be reborn or incarnate in many different forms as a means to experience, learn, evolve, and grow. One can be reborn over and over in a continuous flow from one life to the next. However, rebirth can occur in a time period earlier than the current incarnation. We can incarnate as humans, opposite genders, animals, rocks, plants, amoeba, or elements of the earth. We can be reborn on other dimensions or planets. Rebirth can combine the memories of another person as well as the soul's own memories. Past life memories can contain ancestral DNA memory. What we consider our own past memories can be archetypal content from the collective conscious. This means that many famous people in history serve as models of strength, heroism, integrity, endurance, compassion or evil, and disruption. Our psyche often incorporates these cultural characteristics of these "larger than life" people and we see them as our own past lives. There are many souls who only reincarnate in one culture and one country, or other souls that incarnate all over the world. A soul may continuously incarnate or not incarnate for what in time we would call centuries. While it is hard for us to contemplate, outside of our dualistic and three dimensional world there is no time and no space.

To illustrate our soul changes, I will use the cloud metaphor which is the theme of this book. One of my favorite pastimes is to watch the clouds when walking. It is easy to see how a cloud shifts and changes due to the wind and atmospheric conditions. If we think of ourselves as akin to the cloud, we can understand the constant changeability of the self we call "I."

I recently read a book by Thich Nhat Hahn (Vietnamese Buddhist monk), and found that he also uses the allegory of clouds as an example of impermanence. Although the cloud changes in shape or type and absorbs moisture so that it goes into another form such as rain, it still contains the same elements as it did when it was white and snowy. In a manner of speaking, the cloud still exists although it has changed form. We as beings of consciousness inhabiting a vehicle (our body) created of physical elements change our form moment to moment, minute to minute, lifetime to lifetime. The role of one life merges with roles once played in other lives. Thus we may have a strong attraction to certain music, ways of living, countries, or mannerisms. Each time our soul manifests again into another physical body, it carries a vague awareness of other lives but the body is composed of new genetic materials, physical matter and is impacted by different environmental and cultural influences. Wisps of memory of another life may surface at times with stimulation. The recollection can be a strong one if enough of the same consciousness is interred in a new physical body.

The whole topic of reincarnation, rebirth, and transmigration of the soul or re-embodiment of the soul is complex and would take a book to completely cover all its aspects. However, let's keep it simple and as you read Tom's book on clouds and cloud formations, think of yourself as the ever-changing cloud.

Judith Marie McLean, PhD

Author of:
Ascension Journey, A Handbook for Healing Towards Ascension
available on Amazon.com

Reincarnation of Our Souls

Many people do not believe in reincarnation of the Soul. Given our travels and experiences, Caroline and I firmly believe in our Souls reincarnating time after time, perhaps over thousands of years. In reading the work of Michael Newton, PhD in his book "Journey of Souls," I learned about how he age-regressed thousands of people and many of these people told of past lives in great detail. His book is a well-documented series of case studies which describe what happens to us after we die.

Through our direct experiences, investigation through psychic sessions, and the messages I receive from my Guides and Angels, I have been able to assemble a list of past lives that I have had. It would appear that I was allowed to find these past lives so that I would attempt to retrieve those portions of my Soul Energy left at those locations of my prior deaths by travelling to those places. I would like to share this list with you.

My very first experience, if you can believe it, was inside my mom's womb as a developing baby inside her. I distinctly remember a vision I had that showed me running away from soldiers along with other peasants. The soldiers were killing us with swords and spears. As I was running, I stopped and looked back a second and in that instant a very long spear that was thrown went through me just above the belly button area. It went completely through me and pinned me to the ground where I died. In "Journey of Souls," Dr. Newton describes case studies where someone had a past life with a violent death - say a gunshot to the head - and in this life that person would have a birthmark on the head where that bullet had hit. In my case, I was born with a large hernia in the same spot that the spear entered my abdomen. Additionally, I had at least three lower vertebrae that were malformed or partially formed in the area where the spear came through my back. When I was old enough to talk, I told my mom of this vision, and she did not want to hear any of that at all.

Next is at least two lives as an Aboriginal tribesman in Australia. At least three independent psychics have gotten this information about me in sessions with them. They estimate that this occurred about 5,000 years ago. My friend Alan, when we first met in San Francisco, channeled this information and told me I must go back to Australia sometime.

Another set of past lives occurred around 800 to 500 BC in the area of Naples, Italy. I was a Greek person in those lives and died young in those cases. I had a vision in 2012 sitting in my backyard reading the book "The Atlas of Mysterious Places" when I turned to the page 48 which told of "Cumae - Ancient Cave of Prophecy." That vision directed us to go to Cumae. Cumae was a Greek colony starting about 800 BC in the location of what is now Naples, Italy.

Several psychics have told me that I had several lives during the Roman Empire era of roughly 200 BC to 400 AD.

Another psychic told me that I was a child of a rich family in China or Japan and that I had to sit on a pillow for hours each day with my feet bound. Maybe that life was as a female.

Another past life according to my psychic Francie Marie was as a follower of St. Francis of Assisi during his time on Earth.

According to another psychic, I was a navigator and mapmaker in 1311 in Naples, Italy. Naples was a port city where ships came in to dock from all around the world. Apparently, since I looked to the moon often as a part of my navigator skills, I noticed it was round and then thought why wouldn't the Earth be round too. According to the story, I was murdered with a knife because I could not keep my mouth shut. I was telling people that the Earth was round, when the mainstream thought was that the Earth was flat. Apparently, that was not acceptable to someone.

For several years, Caroline had been suggesting that we take a trip to England and France. I did not want to go to either of those countries, but I especially did not want to go to France. I did not know what it was about France, but I had the worst feelings about France. But in 2008, I agreed to go to England and that led us to go to France.

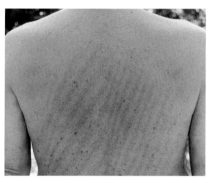

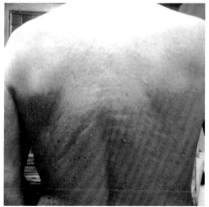

That same year, in a session with Francie Marie prior to our trip, she said my guides were instructing me to take photos of my back each day while I was in France. She said they are going to show you a past life. When we got there, we did take pictures of my back each day while in France. Then one day, the photos showed something weird. Normally, my back is smooth and devoid of any scars or marks other than moles. But this one photo I took with my iPhone showed the left half of my back with a huge curved scar like I had been whipped and the other half with my ribs showing like I was starving to death. Now I had some proof of a past life in the form of photographs.

Later on that trip through France, we were on a train from Paris to the west coast of France. The train slowed and then stopped at a small train station at the town of Dax. As we approached the station, both of my wrists just above the hand began to have intense pain. It felt like long needles were being plunged into each wrist rapidly over and over again. I told Caroline I was in such terrible and incredible pain and what am I going to do. Fortunately, after five minutes, the train left the station and all of a sudden the pain in my wrists was gone like nothing had ever happened. How do you explain that? It was so remarkable an incident, that I called my psychic from France. I asked her if she felt anything about this pain incident. Yes, she said, "During Roman times, you were a person living in France and soldiers captured you and chained you against a wall with your arms overhead. This lasted for days, and then they unchained you and immediately cut off both of your hands at the wrist." The interesting thing was that a year later while watching a show about Julius Caesar when he was a military leader, I learned how he would take over countries through brute force. One tactic he had was to go into the villages of France and call out and capture the men and then cut off their hands at the wrists. The remaining villagers would run to other neighboring villages and tell those people not to fight Julius Caesar because he will do this to you.

A few years ago, I had a vision that I lived in the city of Avignon, in southern France. In that vision, what was shown was a page of photographs – classmates as you might see in a page of your high school yearbook. Was it showing me that I was a high school student at that time in Avignon? The interesting part of this story occurred when we went to Hendaye, France which is located at the border with Spain. We went to see the Great Cross of Hendaye in the town square. This 17th century cross is made of stone and has ancient symbols on it that supposedly tell of a future worldwide catastrophe. As we took photographs of this monument, an older man kept walking back and forth around us and then he stopped to talk. That was hard because we could not speak French or Spanish. So we did the best we could. He persisted in trying to talk to us. I told him that we just came from Avignon. All of a sudden, he gets his wallet out of his back pocket. And then he pulls out a 2 inch by 2 inch photograph of him from his high school yearbook taken in Avignon. Did I have a past life with this man? Was I in high school with him in Avignon. Was there another type of connection? By the way, he refused to allow me to take a picture of him.

My psychic Francie Marie also has told me that Caroline and I have had past lives together in Italy and Ireland. She identified that in the 1700s, we both went to the famous Trinity College in Dublin, Ireland. She said we must go there and walk the university commons area where we often would be together in the 1700s. She said once there we would feel that we were there before. We did go to Dublin and walked the college campus and we did feel exactly that.

I had another session with a different psychic and she identified a life I had in World War I as a spy and that I died in a place of snow. This was verified in a session with Kathleen in a channeled conversation with my Dad.

In a session with Francie Marie, she said I had a life during World War II. Apparently I was a monk or priest at a church in France. I was dedicated to helping to get Jewish children away from the Nazis by hiding them in the church. I was later found and killed for these actions.

Several years ago, I had a vision in the middle of the night. It woke me up and then the vision started. All I saw was two human figures, one a man and the other a woman. But I could tell so clearly what they were wearing including how the buttons were arranged on the woman's dress. They were very well dressed. My feelings were that the clothing looked like what you might expect in the late 1800s. I commissioned an artist to draw this vision and many other visions I had. I told him exactly what I had seen in detail. When he finished with the drawing, I looked up on the internet clothing designs of the 1800s. It was so uncanny! The artist version of the vision precisely showed that the clothing of both people was from the 1897 time in America. Was this Caroline and me in 1897?

Caroline has these feelings as well. She feels a strong connection with the Celtic culture and Ireland. Francie Marie's statement that we both were in Ireland in the 1700s gives that significant credence. On our travels in Ireland and England, she felt a strong connection to many places, including to a holy well in Killarney National Park in Ireland. Also, when we were visiting Stonehenge she felt that she had been in a large procession of people in cloaks walking toward the stones. In that case, she closed her eyes and saw a vision of the procession with many people of that time walking to this sacred site.

In addition, Caroline feels a very strong connection to New York City and the Chrysler Building in the 1920s and 1930s. She feels that she lived and worked there during that time period. When we visited the inside lobby of the Chrysler Building in 2008 we both felt a connection to that era. It was at 5:55 pm on the clock on the wall when we agreed to split up and just walk around inside the beautiful lobby area...perhaps to just touch the walls and entrances, and feel the energy of the place. Twenty minutes later, we got back to together to compare our feelings. It was funny that the first thing we said to each other was that we both felt dizzy for part of the time. Then we both looked up to the clock on the wall. The clock now read 5:11 pm. Somehow we had gone back in time!

No one touched that clock so it had to have gone back on its own. Caroline told me then that she definitely was in that building in the 1920s and she felt that she was waiting for a man at the entrance to 42nd Street for a date. In this life she has such a strong love for the Art Deco art and building architecture, which was so prevalent during that era. Other areas of New York seem to be familiar as well. Also, she has a strong interest in the 1920s of Paris and the French Riviera. When we visited Paris and Nice, France she had strong feelings of knowing those cities and significant buildings which she may have visited in her past life during that time. I always tease her that she must have been very wealthy during that life, since she always seems to have a connection to the best hotels and other locations in these cities.

Getting messages about past lives and actually feeling different about places to which you feel you have a connection occurs for many people. There is that "déjà vu" feeling that many people feel. We believe that these connections somehow bring information and sometimes talents from previous lives to the one that you are currently experiencing. We have both definitely experienced these feelings and messages that we are given. Our interest in these places and time periods have taken us to many places that we might not have otherwise visited and it has enhanced our life immensely.

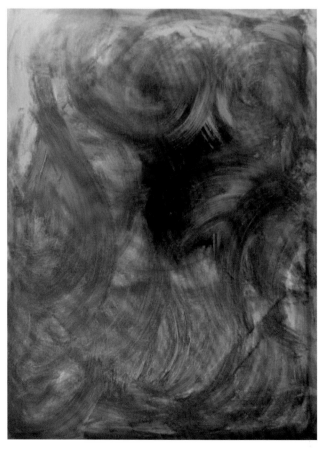

Rebirth

A Constant Connection with My Dad, John Lumbrazo

We all wonder what happens when we die. Some believe there is nothing after death. Some believe we go to Heaven or Hell. There are those who trust that we reincarnate again on Earth at another time. Some have faith that we have a Soul. Some don't believe in a Soul. Our personal experiences are proof to us that there is something quite extraordinary that happens to us when we die or transition into another life.

The story starts with my good friend Judith McLean, who is a very skilled intuitive. She lives in another part of the country. Yet, over the years, we have weekly communication through emails. One day in 2011, I was telling her of the deteriorating health of my Mom and Dad. She responds by saying "Do you want me to check in with your Dad through the higher planes of existence?" I asked "You can do that?" She said "Yes, I can!"

Well, the next day she emailed me and said that my Dad would pass on July 22nd and then your Mom six weeks later. My parents had been married for 64 years. Their passing so close together is similar to the often seen reports in newspapers where this happens to couples that have been together for a long time.

Judith also said my Dad will be met by three of his Italian relatives and my Mom by three Angels. I thought to myself "Is she that good?" It turns out that she is that good.

On July 22nd, I got a call at 9:30 p.m. from the senior care facility where my Dad was staying. He was quite ill with dementia at 92 years old. The staff at the facility told me that I needed to come there right away. So I arrived 15 minutes later and Dad had just passed. He was laying face up in his bed. Suddenly, I got this strange message planted in my mind — "Take a picture of him just above his body!" How weird is that? But I followed the message. So I took a couple of photographs of Dad with my iPhone. I didn't think much of this, since it seemed so crazy. But the next day, I checked those photos. Whoever was talking to me in my mind was right. They wanted me to see his Soul leaving his body. And his Soul was beautiful as you can see here.

The following day, Judith emailed me to say that my Dad, who had just passed, had come to visit her in the night. He told her it was very fuzzy and hard to see in the place that he was in now. He told her that he was visited by three men who he did not know. It sounded like the three men Judith had predicted would appear.

This for me was proof that we don't really die. We move on to another existence, perhaps to another dimension other than our Third Dimension. It is so comforting to know that we do have another life after this one.

The story did not stop there. Dad was a professional trumpet musician. One of the duties he had as a soldier during WWII in Iceland was playing his trumpet for his fellow soldiers and officers. When he came home, he played in bands and even in marching bands. Well, shortly after his death, I began to sing songs without intending to. Day after day, I would be singing songs I had no business singing. And these songs were not of my era, but his era of the 1930s through the 1950s. Clearly, I would not sing these songs on my own.

I could be singing in bed or on a walk with my wife Caroline. Actually, it seemed that any time Dad wanted me to sing, I would sing. He was channeling these songs into me. So Caroline and I began to identify the song titles and look up the lyrics. We wanted to see if Dad was communicating a message to us with these songs. Indeed, he was doing just that!

Dad has been communicating with me in this way since 2011. Even to this very day. Some of the more recent type of songs he downloads into me are:

On December 11, 2016, I was at my computer at 7:30 in the morning and I started singing "It Must Have Been Moonglow" from 1933 by Harry James [a famous trumpet musician] and other artists.

On December 14, 2016, I was in bed with Caroline and I started singing "Has Anybody Seen My Gal" first in 1925 and by many artists through the years.

On January 8, 2017, I was in bed at 11:30 at night and I start singing "I'll Take Manhattan" from 1929 by Rodgers and Hart.

On January 13, 2017, I was outdoors in our backyard with Caroline and we were looking at the bright moon and I began singing "Would You Like to Swing on a Star? Carry Moonbeams Home in a Jar?" by Frank Sinatra and others.

Then there are those from earlier years. This list is a sample of some of the songs he channeled through me in 2013 such as these:

June 6 – "Do You Believe in Magic" by The Lovin' Spoonful

July 3 – "Seasons in the Sun" by Terry Jacks

August 8 – "Rags to Riches"

August 25 – "The Glory of Love" by Peter Cetera

August 26 – "Has Anybody Seen My Gal?"

August 30 – "Way Down Upon the Swanee River"

August 31 – "I'm a Little Teapot Short and Stout"
[This is one my Grandmother would sing to me when I was a child]

September 2 – "Zip-a-Dee-Doo-Dah"

Many times, there would be several songs he channeled to me in one day like these:

September 3 – "The Children's Marching Song", "I Feel Like I'm Fixin to Die Rag" by Country Joe and the Fish, "I Am Off to See the Wizard, the Wonderful Wizard of Oz"

September 4 – "Bye Bye Blackbird", "I'm So Lonesome I Could Cry", "If You Knew Susie, Like I Know Susie, Oh, Oh, Oh What a Gal", "The National Anthem"

Then there was this very special one when Caroline and I were on the island of Oahu, Hawaii in 2014. We were holding hands that morning as we walked an isolated beach on a beautiful day. We were talking about our lives and how much we had accomplished and done over the years. Since we were 66 and 64 at the time, we were reviewing our life I guess. We talked about that fact that we had lived two-thirds of our life so far and if we were lucky, we might have that last third.

All of a sudden, while walking and holding hands with Caroline, I started singing "September Song" by Willie Nelson. Frankly, I don't remember that song he did in 2010 but I sang it like I knew it and then we sang it together, both of us breaking out in tears. As I write this now, I am tearing up.

This song is so special because it is about being together through time and making sure that the last few days of our lives are spent with the knowledge that they are precious. Using the months of the year, the song portrays the phases of our lives from young to old. It tells you when you reach the November of your life, that there are a few precious days left and use the remaining time wisely. To listen to "September Song" and see its lyrics, research it on the internet under "September Song" by Willie Nelson.

Can you imagine all the songs I have been singing since 2011? Hundreds of them! I wish I had a beautiful singing voice to sing them. Dad still gets me to sing two to five times a week. What a special relationship I have with Dad through his songs!

But it does not stop there. Over the last three years or so, the relationship with Kathleen, my therapeutic healing professional, has grown. Specifically, she is able now to access Angels and other Higher Beings while I am laying on her worktable. Guess who she sees come into the room while I am being worked on – Dad! He is there each time I go which is usually once a month. But in addition, Kathleen sees Dad quite often in her home and in the yard. Dad is seen walking down the hallway, and he has even sat down next to Kathleen on her couch. Other people that visit sometimes see him and remark to Kathleen "Who is that little old man?" For you see, Kathleen lives in my parents' house, which is the one that they had before they passed. Dad was so proud of his house in life, and obviously still is proud. Quite extraordinary!

Dad explains that some people can see him now because he had decided to keep his body. I asked him if he was in the fourth dimension. He said no he is not. He said that if you decide to go to the fourth dimension, you no longer have your body. Evidently, he is somewhere between our Third Dimension and the Fourth.

Besides the songs, I am able to communicate with Dad when I am with Kathleen in her home. I can ask him questions and he will respond through her. It is so unique to be able to have such a relationship with your Dad after he has passed. In another section of this book you will be able to read some of Dad's answers to my questions in the section called "Conversations with Dad."

The Afterlife Connection with My Mom, Fern Lumbrazo

Then there is Mom. As you recall, Judith said Fern would pass six weeks after Dad. This is what exactly happened. She died on September 15. The last week of her life was spent in hospice at the senior care facility. The staff had pushed her bed up against the wall just under a very abstract painting I had done for my parents two years earlier.

Each day I would come see her. And I noticed that the painting above her was changing. Now you could see tiny white spots in the center of it. Each day, they would get brighter. Then on the day she died, those white spots turned into the images of three beings.

The day after she died, those beings were gone from the painting. I think Judith was right...she was met with three Angels to assist her death and transition into the next place she was going.

Interestingly, I did not hear from Mom until 2013. One day, my Aunt Myrna called me. She was my Mom's younger sister. We normally would talk a few times a month since she lived in the northeast and I on the west coast. This time she called to ask me to help her fund her new roof and that she would pay us back. Mind you, she would never ask for money so I knew this was hard for her. Anyway, her roof was in terrible condition and she needed a new one. Caroline and I called her back and told her we would mail her a check. Three days later, she got the check and called me so excited because we had told her through a note with the check that it is a gift... not a loan. She was so pleased and we were so happy to help her out.

After the phone call, I went immediately outside. To me the impossible was about to happen. I looked up at the clouds as I always do and saw the impossible! One cloud that appeared to have two large circular eyes was right over our house. I ran into the house to get my camera and when I came back, the left eye had transformed from a circular shape to an absolutely perfect Heart! Unbelievable! If you look closely at the cloud, below the eyes is a horizontal line that sure looks like a bit of a smile on that cloud. That is from my Mom.

I knew that this was my Mom showing me her gratitude and love for what Caroline and I had just done to help her sister. Without a doubt! So you see my Mom was still with me, probably every day like Dad. And she can communicate through the clouds to send a message of love and appreciation.

Mom also shows up when I am having the session with Kathleen. Kathleen usually sees her in the background... not up front like Dad. But I can also talk to her and ask her questions as well. What a special treat to be able to talk to Mom as if she was sitting next to me.

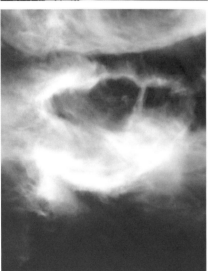

The Afterlife Connection with Caroline's Dad, Harold (Mac) McClure

Caroline and I have been so fortunate to have these experiences with my Mom and Dad. And, by the way, you won't be surprised to learn that Caroline's Dad (Mac) is also with them. Mac passed away in 2012 at 89 years old. A gentle and great man! Mac appeared in 2013 over his home in a cloud image as Caroline was tending to his vacant home. I was fortunately outside and was able to capture his head and face as you can see.

Mac frequently is with my Dad in the sessions with Kathleen. According to them, they spend a lot of time together having fun. According to Dad and Mac, they keep busy doing a lot of the things they used to do here on Earth.

Caroline loved her Dad so much and she really misses him. However, Mac also made another connection with Caroline. An unbelievable one! Totally unexpected!

Later in 2012, the year Mac passed, Caroline and I went out to do some errands. One of the errands was to buy the latest Diana Krall CD named "Glad Rag Doll." After that, we drove to the camera shop and when I got back in our SUV, I asked Caroline to open the cellophane wrapping around the CD. We then opened the plastic case which showed the CD itself and the color booklet that goes with it. We then opened the color booklet. What we saw was unbelievable! This could not be happening!

We thought that the CD booklet was a misprint because it had on each page a dotted like black pattern in the form of a head. We had never seen anything like this before. After focusing on this image, we both immediately said to each other — this is Mac!

In the image, you can see his ears, mouth, and eyes. Without a doubt, they are keenly similar to his face in this life.

Well, it makes such sense to us. Mac just loved Diana Krall and had to have all her CDs. He would play her music all the time. With us buying her latest CD that day, what better way for him to communicate to us through his favorite singer. To us, this was a sign that he is with us and that he loves us. There would not be a better way to show us his presence was still in our lives.

I have a question of Mac...how did you get that image inside the CD with the wrapper around it?

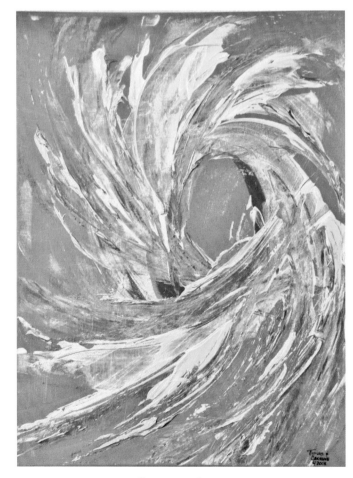

Always with You

Conversations with Dad

John, my Dad, passed away on July 22, 2011. Within days, I started singing songs that were popular in the 1930s, 1940s, and 1950s. It persisted day after day and I began to realize that it had to be coming from Dad. Dad was a trumpet musician so it figured that he would use music to communicate with me. I would sing in bed with Caroline, or walking with her, or biking with her. I would sing immediately upon getting up in the morning or at lunch. It didn't matter.

You could say I am making this up. But I am not. The proof is that I was often singing songs that I never heard of before. Also, I was singing songs of his era, not mine. This has persisted from 2011 to the present day. It has been amazing to have this connection with your parent who has departed from Earth but is still around you like a Guardian Angel.

I remember that about three years ago Dad would appear in my intuitive sessions with our friend Kathleen, who lives in my parents' home now that they are gone. Soon after laying on her massage table, she would say "Your Dad is here!" I would ask her to describe him and she would relate how he is smaller and has that hat on. For me, that confirmed it was Dad.

Kathleen also described how she would see him several times each week roaming the house or even inspecting the backyard. Even some of her friends would come over to Kathleen's and remark "Who is the little man that is walking through the house?"

My intuitive sessions with Kathleen evolved to where I could converse with Dad through Kathleen. One time, Dad told me he wanted to be in this new book I would be writing. I said "Okay, let's do it!" He said a chapter should be called "Conversations with Dad."

So every time I had a session with Kathleen, I would ask Dad several questions that people in general might be interested in. The following is a portion of the compilation of questions I asked Dad from January through April 2017:

Question: Dad, do you remember when I hurried to your Senior Care Facility after I got the call you might pass very soon. When I arrived 15 minutes later, you had just died. Did you see me from your bed after you died? And did you send me the message in my mind to take that photograph just above your body to capture the image of your Soul?

Dad: Yes, I did see you and I did send you that message. It was important.

Question: Where are you now? Are you in the Fourth Dimension since we are in the Third Dimension?

Dad: I am in between. If you proceed to the Fourth Dimension, then you lose your human body. We [Dad and Mac – Caroline's Dad] chose to keep our bodies for now so we did not go all the way into the Fourth Dimension.

Question: How did you know that you could keep your body?

Dad: The answer is within your Soul...you just know your options. There was no need for guidance or assistance.

Question: Do you get any sort of training or guidance where you are?

Dad: No. I get to do whatever I want to do. I have complete freedom to choose. There is unbelievable Love and Peace here. It is so beautiful here and the colors of everything are so much brighter.

Question: Do you ever feel drained of your energy or need a recharge of your energy?

Dad: No, never! I don't need that at all.

Question: When you look around you now, what do you see?

Dad: I see the same things you see my son. But I see them with much more enhanced color.

Question: Do you rest or sleep?

Dad: Yes, I do! I can take a nap or sleep whenever I want. However, I do not eat as it is not necessary.

Question: Where is our 20-year-old cat Tigger now that he just died?

Dad: He is with me now along with your other cats that have passed. Kathleen can see them around me and in my lap. Tigger sends his Love and Gratitude. He thanks you for including him in the book.

Question: So you have a lot of cats with you! Do the cats where you are chase birds and rats?

Dad: Yes they do son! But they don't kill anything.

Question: Often Kathleen sees you and Mac [Caroline's Dad] together in these sessions. What do you guys do?

Dad: We chose to be together and we are good friends. We have tons of fun playing cards together. By the way, Mac said to tell Caroline that he loves her and is grateful for her. You know, we can do whatever we want here. I see many of my friends from my days on Earth and we meet, talk, and have fun together. All the stuff we could do on Earth.

Question: Do you ever get together with other people up there to form a group that works together to solve a problem or achieve a goal?

Dad: Yes, we sometimes get together to do something to help save the Earth.

Question: Have you helped anybody else on Earth besides me?

Dad: I have gone to many people on Earth and whispered in their ear or sang to them.

Question: Did we have past lives together and reincarnated"

Dad: Yes, we did. We had those two lives in Siracusa, Sicily long ago and of course our lives together in this time.

Question: Do you know how many past lives or reincarnations I have had on Earth?

Dad: Son, you have had thousands of lives on Earth over thousands of years. Too many to count!

Question: I resonate with Lions. Did I ever have a life as a Lion?

Dad: Yes, you did son. [At that moment, Kathleen sees a vision of me as that lion perched on a hill and with a very dark mane.]

Question: Do you have Peace where you are now?

Dad: Yes, I do. And I have the emotions you have like laughing, joy, and happiness.

Question: Do you have a form of intimacy or sex where you are now?

Dad: Not the kind that you have on Earth. But we have other forms of gratification.

Question: Do you know if you will reincarnate again on Earth?

Dad: No, I don't want to! Son, many people reincarnate on Earth to experience living in a third dimensional world with all its solid objects, and to experience the emotions of being a human being. Most of the people on Earth today have been reincarnated.

Question: Are you the one who keeps waking me up at 3:30 or 4:00 in the morning?

Dad: Yes, I have to get you up to work at that new book. After this book, you will do a series of other books.

Question: Michael Newton, PhD in his book "Journey of Souls" talks about each of us on Earth belonging to a Soul Group and that we reincarnate with members of that Soul Group. How many Souls are there in your Soul Group?

Dad: I don't know exactly but it is a very huge number. So many I cannot count them.

Question: Recently, a psychic told me I had a prior life in World War I two lifetimes ago. True?

Dad: Yes, you had a life in World War I. You were a spy of some sort who gets killed. I am not sure where it was but you were in an area of a lot of snow. Something might happen in this life as a result of that life.

Question: About two years ago, Kathleen started seeing in our sessions eight Italian relatives of ours lined up behind you in a row. What was that about?

Dad: Yes, son, that is true. They were our Italian relatives that have passed on. They all had Karma that had to be released. You had to go to Siracusa, Sicily to remove it. Now, we are all released from Karma and are grateful for you and Caroline for helping us. You were chosen because you and Caroline decided not to have children so you are the end of the blood line. You had to do this!

Question: Were you assigned to help me and Caroline here on Earth?

Dad: I chose to help you and to do my part to help save the Earth.

Question: Do you see Angels where you are?

Dad: Yes, I can talk to them and the Archangels. You know, like Archangel Michael...and the whole cast of characters.

Question: Do you get to see Mom?

Dad: Yes, sometimes I see her.

Question: Have you connected with your Mom and Dad?

Dad: Yes, I have seen my Dad Theodore. I have also seen my sister Ann, your Aunt Ann.

Question: Do you plan to stay around me until I die?

Dad: Yes, I do son. And I plan to help you with your next book and your travels.

Question: Do you remember that trumpet playing that beautiful song on that night of April 19, 2012 in my backyard?

Dad: Yes son, that was me playing for you on what would have been my and your mom's 65th anniversary.

Question: You seem to have an affinity towards Kathleen who is next to me. What's up?

Dad: Well, I am the one that got Kathleen to decide to rent and stay in our home in 2012 so that this channeling could happen.

Question: Any more about this book I am writing?

Dad: Yes, it is important that you include photos of you and Caroline growing up and our family. It is also important that you include photos in the new book that came from your first three books. And also include a section on the family values of the era of the 1950s.

Question: Why did I have that vision and pass out reading that book "The Atlas of Mysterious Places?"

Dad: Yes, you had to go to Naples, Italy to see the Cumaen Sibyl's home. You had to retrieve parts of your Soul that were left in that spot when you had several Greek lives hundreds of years before Christ. You died very young there.

Question: I think I have had experiences where the people I meet seem to be Angels to give me a message? You know, Angels in human form. Is this true?

Dad: Yes, son, Angels can come to Earth in human form. You had that experience where a woman you did not know came to you two months after your car accident in 2001. She told you your life would be changing and to journal everything each day as you would forget many things if you didn't. You also had that experience where two women met you and Caroline in Monument Valley and Sedona, Arizona to give you the message of Divine Love.

Question: Many people talk about these Orbs that show up in photographs...you know those circular bubbles in the air. What are they?

Dad: Orbs are people and animals that have passed on and they can be various sizes and colors.

Question: Some say that money will be obsolete in the future and bartering will be the thing to do. What do you think?

Dad: Yes, it is true. In the future, those people that store gold will be very surprised as it will have no value. What will be valuable will be water, food, and air.

Question: Does evil try to get into the place you reside now?

Dad: Yes, it does. But it is repelled and protected by the purity and goodness of this place.

Question: Are there evil people where you are like there are here on Earth?

Dad: Yes, son, there is evil in the various realms of existence. For example there are good and bad aliens some of which are on Earth now. The Sirians, Pleiadians, and Arcturians are good. The evil aliens are battling to keep the control of the Earth they have now. There is an even bigger war in the Highest Realms...a battle of Good vs Evil and of Light vs Dark. This battle for the Earth is so very important to the Higher Realms in order to succeed in keeping the Light.

Question: You said that aliens are already here. Any more information?

Dad: Aliens have been here a long time. They have had ships coming out of the oceans. Soon people will be able to see them. Some malevolent aliens from another galaxy have discovered the Earth and want to control it but some benevolent aliens are also here and are trying to protect us. There is a Grid around the Earth helping to protect us and our planet. People must do their part in protecting the Grid by praying or visualizing the Grid or the Hands of God holding the Earth. More and more people are awakening on Earth to this need and it must continue.

Question: Dad, it is now April 25th, 2017. I have one more week to complete the draft of this book. This morning as I was working on the book, I was researching internet sites about Archangel Michael. All of a sudden, a pornographic site full of large nasty photographs of naked people pops up on my computer screen. There was no identification of the site and a box in the center said this may be a virus and wanted me to push OK. I felt this was too strange and I was able to remove it about 20 seconds without pushing OK. Was this an attack by the unseen evil forces on our book so it would be delayed or destroyed?

Dad: Yes, son it was a deliberate attack on the book. When and if this happens again, ask for Archangel Michael to stop the attack at its source.

Question: Do you have a message for people on Earth?

Dad: Yes I do. Stop what you are doing! Stop destroying the Earth, the animals and plants.

Question: You know that many people on Earth are searching for the meaning of life. What is the meaning of life?

Dad: LOVE is the answer for the meaning of life on Earth and in the Higher Realms.

Dad Trumpeted His Love for Mom

My Dad passed in July 2011. Six weeks later my Mom passed in September 2011. They had been married for 64 years. They were always together each day and supported each other in so many ways. They were married on April 19, 1947 in upstate New York.

After Dad passed, I started getting all kinds of messages from him. Mostly his messages would be in the form of music. He would channel into me and I would start singing a song that he wanted. But there were other messages as well. This next message is so very special.

Dad was a professional trumpet musician from his 20s until his 50s. You would figure that his messaging to us might be in the form of music. The following year after my parents' deaths, Caroline and I were sitting in our backyard late in the afternoon. I recall we were having a glass of wine together on our outside deck. This deck faces a beautiful open field of about 40 acres filled with mature oak trees and natural grasses. It was always so quiet and peaceful.

As the sun was going down, we were talking about how last year was so hard for us due to the loss of my parents. Then in the still of the dusk of that night, a lone trumpet played loudly. We looked around our house and our neighboring houses. We looked into the field. There was no one in sight. We certainly did not see anyone with a trumpet.

The music was a song we had never heard but it reminded us of that time in the 1940s when music was so beautiful and special with the big bands. The trumpet continued to play. After eliminating all the possible sources of it, it became clear to us that it was from Dad. Without a doubt, that sound was emanating from that field. We had never heard of any similar music from the field for the 33 years we had been living at this location. Who else could be playing a trumpet in our field?

Then we just sat back and enjoyed the song. We thought of Dad playing his lone trumpet in his distinctive style. The song touched us! You could feel the Love coming out of that horn.

Then it occurred to us what was happening. It was April 19, 2012! It was the 65th wedding anniversary of Mom and Dad even though they were no longer with us. It was John, my Dad, honoring his wife Fern, and sending his Love to Mom via the horn. At that moment, we realized we just witnessed an incredibly special event that most people never get to experience. The expression of Love from the Afterlife! And he allowed us to be a part of it.

Dad Wants Us to Remember the 1950s

As I was conversing with my Dad recently through Kathleen, Dad asked me to communicate in this book how much people and our society have changed since the 1950s. His point is that we should reflect on some of the things that had great value in the 1950s.

We had a population nearing 180 million in 1960, but today we are near 325 million.

I remember we seemed to show more respect for others, such as saying "Sir" to someone rather than to just say "Hey" or "Dude." How did we lose that?

Also it seems with the advent of advanced technology we seem to have forgotten the art of sending people "Thank You" cards or notes after receiving a gift or when a favor was done. A "thank you" sent by email just doesn't seem as personal as a handwritten note or card. Often, nothing of any kind is received. What are people thinking when they don't respond back with kindness?

I remember we used to be more formal and tied to long-standing traditions like opening the door for another person or woman at a building or a car. Where did our respect and courtesy for other people go?

It also seems that we have lost courtesy and respect in many aspects of our country. For example, "dressing up" nicely to go out. Today a lot of people dress in the most shabby clothes to go out in public or even to what are special events such as parties, shows, weddings, and even going to church. It is not like most people don't have money to purchase clothes in this most abundant country with so many malls full of clothing stores.

As a child, I remember my friends and I could play outdoors all day long and not have to worry about being abducted or having our moms hover over us. Today, children seem to have to play in structured activities and many children are indoors so much playing with their phones, computers, play stations, or watching TV. You seldom see unaccompanied children at stores or even around the neighborhood. There is a lot of fear in the country and that might explain some of this but also we seem to be more distracted with gadgets than to relate to other people.

Caroline and I are always amazed to see two or more people seated at a restaurant with them looking at their smart phones yet not communicating with each other. Caroline and I were taught to respect others at the dinner table or in a restaurant when dining.

It seemed that there was more respect for our institutions of government, schools, churches, and other organizations. Whereas today, people seem to be in disarray about our government representatives and there seems to be a lack of respect for them. In today's world, even our government leaders and representatives engage in name calling and perhaps worse.

Remember when high school football players graduated, they just silently went on to college or the work world. Today, the better high school football players gather together with TV coverage to announce what college they decided to go to. Yet, the best high school academic graduates get little or no coverage about what college they selected and what they have accomplished.

You could leave your home for hours or days and not lock the doors and everything would be still there when you got back. When did people decide it was not safe to leave their homes unlocked? Of course today, we have the additional protection of alarm systems.

You had much more privacy. Hardly anyone would be able to steal your Social Security number or bank information. Now, all of our privacy is gone especially with regard to Social Security numbers, driver's licenses, credit cards, and other personal information including emails and photographs. Our computers and mobile phones are a blessing, but they easily get hacked by anyone in the world resulting in the loss of our most private information. In addition, our identities can be hacked. Even we can be spied on through mobile phones and TVs. Most everyone now seems to accept this huge loss of privacy as normal!

You used to be able to copyright your creative products like books, movies, paintings, etc. and feel very protected from criminal theft. Now a copyright has less value or is worthless since so many people steal these products and feel no remorse in taking photographs of someone else's art work, copying movies, or finding ways to steal cable systems with no regard for compensating those who created and owned these products. Their belief system seems to be "Free is always good especially if you don't get caught!" How did we get to this point in our society?

I remember people seemed to be more responsible for what they did. However in today's world, you read almost every day in the news about people who caused a car accident and never stopped, including when they killed someone. Many people seem to have lost the courage to be responsible for their actions or even what they say. What has happened to our character?

In the 1950s, people used to say "Please" and "Thank You" all the time. Now it is more rare to hear it.

You have to wonder why in the 1950s married people rarely divorced and society frowned upon divorce. Now divorce is so commonplace that about half of marriages result in divorce. It is so much more acceptable in society. In many cases marriage seems to be viewed by many people as a date or just a temporary arrangement. If you change your mind then you can discard your partner whenever you want. There seems to be very little commitment to a partner or even children of the marriage.

I remember when you would drive out in the countryside and enjoy the landscape that had farms with horses, cows, goats, sheep, and pigs having the freedom to roam the pastures. Today we have corporate farms where animals are kept in buildings and caged all in the name of higher profits. It seems instead of respecting animals, we now fill them with hormones, medicines, and foods that are supplemented with fillers. What is our future looking like in agriculture if we are headed towards 10 billion people on this planet?

I remember when our farms produced their crops more naturally, and today incredible amounts of pesticides and herbicides are applied to them. So who is protecting us from these pollutants in today's world?

Today there are so many people sick with cancers or other major illnesses, including very young children, as compared to the 1950s when these diseases seemed so much more rare. It is sad that so many people have to endure this pain and suffering, perhaps unnecessarily.

In the 1950s, there was the beginning of the development of freeways. The amount of traffic you would normally encounter was generally minor to moderate. Today, our cities are booming as major regions of population and cars. As a result, our roads and freeways are so congested that it takes so much more time to get home from work or school. Now we spend our time on the freeways rather than spend it with our families.

It is interesting to reflect upon what we had in the United States in the 1950s. Gone are the days of more freedom and privacy. We had less fear of crime and violence. We felt more safe in our homes, towns, and cities. Perhaps we were more close to each other through our friends and families, small towns and cities. We had better food and diets. And it seemed that we had more time.

In summary, I think Dad wanted to convey the huge differences in our society from not so long ago. He wanted us to reflect on these differences and to decide what kind of life and society we want in the future.

Reflection

May the Clouds Bless You!

Chapter 4

The Magic Within the Clouds

Be a rainbow in someone's cloud!
— Maya Angelou

This Chapter is about the clouds above us. There are very special clouds in the sky for each of us if we only look. The clouds are no different than the messages we all receive from Angels and family and friends that have passed on to another realm of existence.

Caroline and I have been fortunate to be able to resonate with clouds over the last few years. We had so many special cloud images that we wrote three books about them. The messages from the clouds still come to us, to guide us, to amaze us, and to show their sheer beauty.

The clouds can awaken each of us to the reality of our existence on Earth. They can cause us to reflect on their beauty and wisdom. How they transform to create these incredible images is perhaps a secret they want to conceal for now. All Caroline and I know is that they are real, they exist in our reality on Earth, and it is important to honor them just as we might honor all of the God's creations.

After the Epilogue section of this book, there are many special clouds presented as well. They are called "Clouds that Remind Us of Angels," "Clouds that Remind Us of Animals," and "The Orchestra of Clouds." Caroline and I have prepared suggested meditations for these clouds for you to use and enjoy.

There Is Magic Within the Clouds

Most of us think of clouds in a very positive way. They are beautiful, fluffy, and white, and also gray with the life-sustaining water resulting from the rain and snow within them. When as children, we fondly remember looking up and thinking we saw an image of an Angel or animal in a cloud. As adults, we usually take the clouds for granted as a part of our natural landscape each day.

Through my research on Wikipedia, I found that a man named Paracelsus, born in Switzerland on November 11, 1493, termed a mythological spirit of the air as a Sylph. In his works, he describes Sylphs as invisible beings or elementals of the air. Today, Sylphs are generally described as minor spirits, elementals, or faeries of the air. So did Paracelsus actually see the spirits in the air? Unfortunately, he did not have a modern camera to capture those images to show us.

As I have mentioned before, I started seeing Cloud Spirits or Sylphs starting in November 2007 when Caroline and I went to Peru. On our train to Machu Picchu, I saw the Condor Cloud, the Puma Cloud, and at Puno on Lake Titicaca, I saw the Snake Cloud. All of those were the three Inca Gods. It did not stop there. I became more aware of these Cloud Spirits and looked in earnest everyday for them.

Amazingly, something so incredible happened about five years ago when I was with a psychic I had not used before. That day as our session proceeded, she described that she was feeling a lot of pressure in her forehead. She then told me something wanted to come into our space and talk to us. I agreed.

As she channeled that Being, he came in and said his name was King Paralda. He said he was the King of the Element of Air, Clouds or the Cloud Spirits. He said that he works under the jurisdiction of Archangel Raphael, his Master. I had never heard of this before. He went on to say he was pleased with my work photographing clouds but expressed concern about the Earth. He said he was concerned about the future of the Earth, and as a result, of his Cloud "people." He wondered if He and the Cloud Spirits would survive? He wanted me to know this so that I might be able to help.

I then researched Wikipedia again on the subject of King Paralda. According to this research, King Paralda is real. He is King of the Air Element, which is one of the four Elements of Air, Water, Earth, and Fire. As you probably are aware, these four Elements are necessary for all life on Earth. Without them, we could not exist like we do today or exist at all.

I have to be honest with you that if you told me that there is a King Paralda, I certainly would have some doubts. Perhaps I would call you crazy. But in my case, I have talked to him through the channeling of my psychic. I have no doubts now.

Some people say they can create the images of Cloud Spirits or Sylphs just by thinking of the image in their mind. I think that is true. I think it is possible that our mental thoughts can be received by the Sylphs which can result in them trying to message us by forming a cloud in that image. There is a cloud later in this chapter that shows the image of Santa Claus on his sleigh. My Dad, after his passed, said that he created that for me to see and to take photographs of it.

Think about it…if King Paralda is real, then you have to realize that there may be consciousness in the clouds similar to the consciousness we all have. I have come to realize this very fact. The cloud images in this chapter are extraordinary. They don't represent the image of clouds we see on an everyday basis. They are unique and special.

Caroline and I are so blessed to be able to show you the cloud images we have captured with our camera. I have focused on Cloud Spirits that are very positive energy beings. I have to be honest with you and tell you that I have also captured images of negative or even evil Cloud Spirits. Just like us, the good and evil exists in the sky as well. I have even been attacked by some evil Cloud Spirits when their image comes on the computer screen. The attack has been in the form of severe pain in my forehead. I know that this is true because immediately after I remove that image on the computer screen, the pain stops instantly.

With each Cloud Spirit photograph, there will either be a story attached to it or a Meditation suggested by me that you might utilize for yourself. Remember that whatever you see in the clouds is your interpretation…it is what you see. No one has the right to criticize your interpretation or dispute what you see. In fact, I find that usually each Cloud Spirit image actually contains several Cloud Spirits. In other words, in many cases the overall image might be made by several Cloud Spirits coming together.

We hope you enjoy "The Magic Within The Clouds!"

On the Wings of Angels

Many people look at the clouds and see Angels or Angelic Beings. There have been several songs created with this theme of "On the Wings of Angels."

One afternoon, I took this photograph when this cloud came over our house. Not only did it appear to be very angelic with its wings, but it was so huge in the sky. It covered nearly one-half of the visible sky. When I loaded the photo into my computer, there was no question what it was, and that it was so special. As you look at it, you can see it represents angel wings and notice the right wing is bent to imitate angel wings like you might see in books and paintings of angels.

So we have picked this very special photograph to begin this chapter about clouds and cloud messages.

The Goddess Who Heals

In May 2009, I was taking photographs of clouds outside my home. Sometimes I get some excellent cloud images near the sun. On this day, something very special was close to the sun. As I looked through my camera lens, I saw an image of what looked like a human figure, but I could not make it out. So I just took several photographs. Later I loaded them on my computer and then I realized these images were so incredible.

From my interpretation, the human-like figure is a female who has her hand over a smaller being. It appears that she is healing that child-like figure. She also looks to be very powerful in her abilities. So that is why I named her "The Goddess Who Heals." You certainly never know what you might discover in our skies.

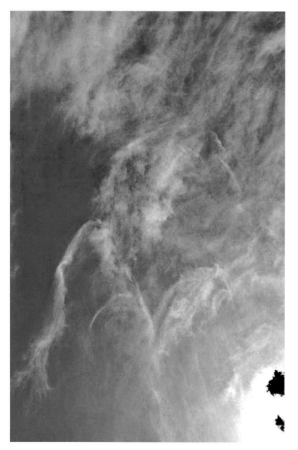 

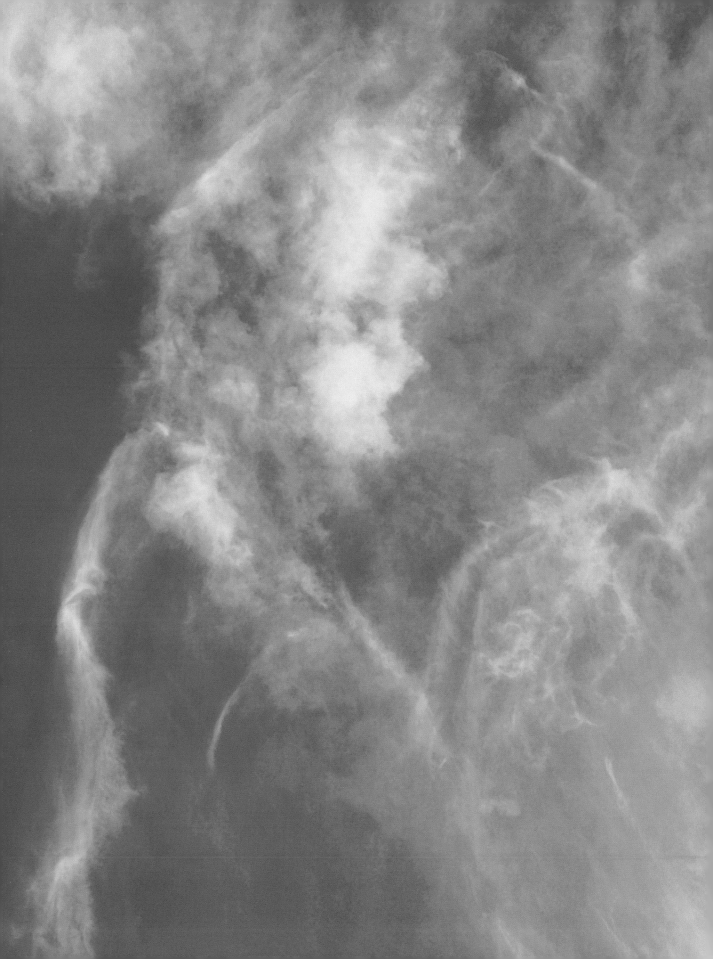

"I Am So Sorry, for You Need This Gift!"

In 2005, after over a year of being attacked by one or more evil spirits, I became so depressed and angry. I could find no cure for eliminating these evil spirits. They were attached to me and I could actually feel and see them and it felt like they were taking over my body.

One day I was especially depressed. More than any other day in my life! I felt helpless. I took a short drive alone and after some thought, I summoned my courage and declared that I would not cave in to those evil spirits. I would fight them every way I could no matter what.

When I got home, I found a message on my business phone. When I played it, I could not believe what I was hearing. I kept playing it over and over as it seemed so unreal. The message was **"I AM SO SORRY, FOR YOU NEED THIS GIFT!"** The background of the message was scratchy but there was an angelic sound of music in the background. It was clearly a female voice and she was singing this message. It felt so much like it came from another place other than Earth.

Then I found that there were five more messages on the phone. This time they were from a male voice over and over again, five times. The message was very rapid. It was **"EVERYTHING WILL BE ALRIGHT!"**

I asked Caroline to come into my office to hear these messages. She said I was not crazy. These were real. After some discussion, I went outside. It was near sunset and I noticed some clouds near the horizon. I went back inside to get my camera. Then I took several photographs of what appeared to be unusual clouds.

When I pulled those photographs up on my computer, I was a bit stunned. They showed a precise image of what appears to be a female-looking cloud being with her hand out and in her hand is a triangular object like a pyramid.

Later, I showed this photograph to my psychic Francie Marie. Instantly, she said that the female cloud being was a woman who had lived on Earth and had become so depressed she committed suicide. She added that the woman was expressing her regret for that decision and as a message to me to not decide to do something you will regret.

I then played those voice mail messages. Francie Marie confirmed that the voice of the female was the same as the female in the cloud. It became apparent to me at that moment that these messages and cloud were a sign from above for me to fight this depression I was having and to have the courage, patience, and persistence to beat these evil spirits. I have never looked back after that day. So you see, you never know when the messages will come to you and in what form but it is important to see and to listen. I feel so blessed to have been a part of this event.

The Shaman Comes in a Cloud

When our first book, "The Journey to the Clouds," was delivered to our house, it was certainly a very special day for us. As you can imagine, seeing that huge truck come and deliver a pallet of hundreds of books, it felt like a "birth" was taking place. It took many months to take all the photographs, write the book and edit it, and then to wait for the copies to be printed. Finally it arrived and we were so happy.

At that moment, as always, I was looking to the sky and the clouds. Just above the horizon and over the sun, I saw a very different kind of cloud. It looked like a bubble. So I took some photographs and later on my computer, I saw the results. It was a bubble like I saw, but it had a human-like figure inside it. That figure reminded me of images I had seen of a native Shaman, with a headdress of what appears to be deer antlers. The Shaman appears to be dancing to the music of the drum beating. Why this kind of cloud now for me to see? Perhaps the Shaman was honoring the completion of the book! I would like to think so.

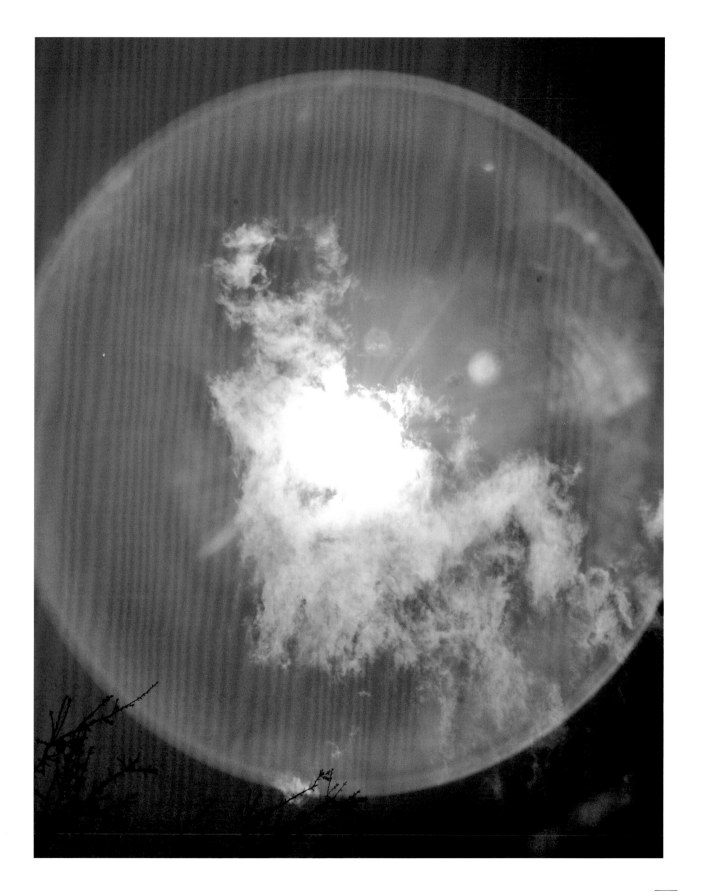

Our Sweet Cat "Sassy" Says Goodbye

Caroline and I love animals. We feel that they are one of the things that makes our planet so special. When they are part of our lives, they bring love and joy. What would our world be like if we did not have them?

We have had many cats in our lives. The last few years, over a period of time, we had up to six cats at our home. All of them were strays that came to us one by one. One of them was a small calico feline we named "Sassy." She always wanted her way. The other five cats were male and much larger. However, she was clearly the boss of those cats. If any of them got too close to her, she would swat them in the face.

She was a delight to have in our home and we loved her so much. So it was hard to see her deteriorate as she got older. She was thirteen when she started failing badly and we took her to the veterinarian to assess her status. In our car on the way to the veterinarian, Caroline was holding her in her lap, comforting her. As Caroline sat in the veterinarian's office chair, Sassy passed away peacefully in her arms.

While it is always a sad time to experience a favorite pet passing, this time it was different because Sassy passed so peacefully and with the love that Caroline was giving her.

Well, that could be the end of this story! But it is not. Since I watch the skies so frequently for messages from the clouds, I was a bit surprised three days later. I was outside in our backyard, when suddenly there was a small cloud over our house. It just stayed there. I ran into the house to get my camera and quickly took a photograph of this cloud. It was definitely a cloud in the image of a cat. As you can see by the photograph, the outline of the cloud has the face, eyes, and ears like a cat, and also that large cat-like rear foot. This cloud was different in that it did not change form and lasted several minutes while other clouds passed by.

In my mind, I said "That is Sassy!" She had come to say goodbye to us, to say she loved us, and that she is okay. What a special time to have a loved one, be it a person or animal, come back after death to make such a connection with those that are living.

Well, it does not stop there. I have therapeutic healing sessions frequently with our friend Kathleen, and the following year Sassy appears again. Many times during these sessions with Kathleen, there is often a spiritual component where she sees angels come into the room along with a cast of other spiritual beings. Kathleen was telling me at this time that she was channeling a number of our cats that had passed away. And she saw Sassy, this time sitting on my Dad's lap who passed in 2011. At that point I asked my Dad through Kathleen why he had a cat on his lap since he was not that fond of cats. He said, "Tom, it is different here, it is about Love."

Caroline and I have had so many experiences like this where there is a communication between us and the departed. Generally speaking, all of us are taught not to believe in this, but for us it is very true. We have no doubt that there is communication with the beings in our lives that have now passed on.

The Young Girl that Came to Say "Thank You"

A friend called me one day in 2009 and asked if I could come to the hospital and help her teenage daughter, Her daughter was dying of an advanced form of cancer. I immediately went to the hospital to console her and to do what I could.

I had studied how we humans can send our energy into others who need healing. Some call this Reiki Energy Healing. I call it Healing with Universal Energy. You see, all of us are Energy. Apparently, we can direct this energy to help people and animals. Perhaps even to heal our planet, which definitely needs it.

The young girl was in a fetal position in her hospital bed when I first saw her. She was connected with every tube and wire imaginable. It made me cry to see her like that! I spent 90 minutes with her that day doing what I could to help. I prayed for her.

One week later, she was doing visibly better. I spent another 90 minutes with her sending positive and healing energies from me. I hoped that she would continue to improve. I called her mom after another week. She told me that her daughter had passed a few days earlier after chemotherapy. It was so sad. I was depressed that she had died. She was so young, intelligent, and had so much to contribute to the world.

Two weeks later, I was in my back yard taking photographs of clouds. Then this really clear and precise cloud came over my house and stayed in the same exact location for over 20 minutes. I watched it stay in the same place as other clouds passed by. Of course, at the same time I was taking lots of photographs of it.

Later as I looked at these photographs in detail on my computer, I noticed how incredibly it matched the appearance of the young girl I had spent all that time with in the hospital.

That cloud image was almost identical to her. The cloud image had her short hair, her little nose, her face and eye. Of course as I always do, I consulted one of my psychics about what this cloud was. I took this photograph to Francie Marie and she immediately said that her guides were telling her that this indeed was that same young girl that died. But why?

Francie Marie went on to say that the young girl had come to say "Thank You" for my efforts at her bedside and to send her Love. At that moment, I felt this was just another instance of Love crossing the barriers of time and space and between our Third Dimension and the Afterlife. I was so grateful for this whole experience. I will never forget this young girl.

Guided By The Ant People

In 2008, Caroline and I were reading about places to go in the American Southwest in the states of Arizona and New Mexico. One day, I found an article on the Native American Hopi People who have lived for thousands of years in the Southwest desert in Arizona.

According to their legends, the Hopi were saved from a global cataclysm such as an ice age and/or global flood. I did a lot of research on this subject because I was amazed and curious as to how they survived such a calamity.

According to the legends and teachings of the Hopi, they were saved by the Ant People. The Ant People were said to possibly be Extraterrestrials. Apparently, the Hopi were guided by a cloud that led them to the Ant People. The Ant People then took the Hopi to their subterranean caves where there was refuge and food. The Ant People continued to help them by teaching the Hopi how to grow food in the caves and store it.

Two days after reading about the Hopi, I was outdoors taking pictures of clouds and found some very special ones. When I downloaded the photographs on my computer, I found several that looked like Ants. Can you believe it? Ants! As you can see, these Ant creatures or Ant people in the cloud images below are very much like our ants. Very thin in places like the legs and body, and they even had claw-like hands. So how do you explain that I am reading about

the Ant People and then I soon see Ant People in the clouds? Just amazing to ponder isn't it!

That is not the only thing to ponder. We were researching all of this because we wanted to go to Arizona in 2008. On our trip we stopped off in Flagstaff, Arizona which is a very beautiful university town in the mountains of northern Arizona. We were looking at houses and neighborhoods there and we stopped at one and walked through the neighborhood. The homes were newer and the yards consisted of rock or stone and shrubs and trees. As I was walking, my eye caught the appearance of a very special rock...a brown, triangular rock. I picked it up and looked at it. How many triangular rocks with five sides have you seen? And this rock had black images on all its five sides.

In looking closely at this special rock, in my opinion you can see quite clearly the image of the Kachinas which were the Gods of great power to the Hopi. The other image appears to reflect the Kokopelli, a God worshipped by Southwestern Native Americans. How do you explain these images that are clearly more than coincidence? See the images of the rock below.

Obviously this whole story is about guidance, which can come in many forms. In this case we were guided to read about the Southwest, then about the Hopi, and then guided by the clouds to see the Ant People, and finally, to actually be in the Southwest and find this simply amazing rock with the Native American images all over it. I believe we were being led to explore and understand the Hopi and the other Native American peoples, and their legends, and prophecies. Incidentally, is this perhaps a warning to all of us of a future similar global event or calamity? Were we guided by the Ant People themselves? Or simply to educate us that there is more to our life and planet than we are told!

The Message of The Tree of Life

We went to Egypt in 2008 to explore many of the ancient sacred sites and temples. One of the interesting things we noticed was the depiction of The Tree of Life in some of the buildings. Of course, that made us think about why that was so important.

The Tree of Life is seen in many cultures. Trees represent life, protection, shade, and food. We really did not think about it again until 2011 when the sky presented us with a gift.

In November 2011, a special cloud came as I was gazing at the sky. It was tiny so I had to zoom in with my camera. Then I realized it was the image of a tree. Imagine, a tree being represented in the form of a cloud. It had many limbs and branches just as a tree. It was "The Tree of Life" in cloud form!

I really don't know the precise message for it showing up that day in the clouds. But I like to believe that it was conveying a message of the beauty of Life, and to respect and honor it for it sustains us. It resonated with me so much that I had to paint my version of "The Tree of Life."

Hands of God

In June 2011, I woke up on a beautiful summer morning and went outdoors with my coffee to read the paper. As I sat on our large deck outdoors, I noticed how clear and blue the sky was – not a cloud anywhere to be seen.

As I was reading the paper, all of a sudden, there was a voice in my left ear so clear. It was like I was talking to someone next to me. The voice said so simply "LOOK UP NOW!" I have gotten used to this kind of thing so I wondered where to look. I looked immediately over my left shoulder. To my surprise, I saw these two clouds, side by side, that were the image of giant hands and arms. I was so amazed and excited, I ran into the house to get my camera and took several pictures. The hands were so precisely done and formed. What did it mean?

There could be many meanings I guess, but to me it is a comfort to know that these gigantic hands are there to comfort you and me. Or maybe it is to show us that there is a loving presence on this planet. Nonetheless, it was a wonderful experience about the Magic in our lives.

Santa Claus Comes to Town

Caroline and I went to a children's fundraiser about ten miles from our house in the beginning of July 2011. As we came to the event and parked the car, we both got out and Caroline noticed a strange cloud in the north sky. It was small and fuzzy. I quickly got my camera out of the car and pointed it at this cloud and zoomed in with my telephoto lens.

I couldn't believe my eyes! It was a cloud in the image of Santa Claus in a fuzzy hat in a sleigh and a couple of reindeer. I could tell instantly it was Santa! Most of all, his hat was that distinctive Santa Claus hat.

It was so amazing to see this in the sky – Santa Claus! I would have never dreamed this could happen in a million years. I took as many pictures as I could before the cloud evaporated in about five seconds. As you can imagine, Caroline and I couldn't stop talking about this cloud the rest of the day.

Later that year, I had the idea to make the Santa photographs into a Christmas card. I enlarged the images and made a Christmas card with the words on the front "Do you believe in Santa Claus?" and on the back are photos of Caroline and I at three years old. This side of the card said "WE STILL DO!" We ordered 1,000 copies and also emailed it all around.

We emailed this Christmas card and its story to many of the large media outlets, television stations locally and nationally, as well as large newspaper outlets in the country, with no response. All of them probably thought we were crazy or that we PhotoShopped the images.

We also emailed the card to all of our friends. At Christmas time, we would take copies of it and walk down the sidewalk in our town or go into a store and go up to people and say, "Do you believe in Santa Claus?" Amazingly, 99% of these people said, "Yes." We would then give them a copy of the Santa card. All the people that saw it were so excited and so happy to see confirmation that there truly might be a Santa Claus for all of us.

To both of us, Santa Claus is a form of an angel who brings joy and happiness to so many around the world each year. We are so happy that we were able to capture this special cloud for many to enjoy. Perhaps it proves that there is truly Magic around all of us.

The Eagle Cloud Came Through a Vision

One early morning in February 2010, I was awakened and then immediately closed my eyes to see a vision being presented to me. It was very much like a movie and it was about Eagles.

The vision showed me walking up to the front porch of my home and as I looked to the left, I noticed a small hole in the ground near our home's foundation. I felt it was nothing serious and ignored it as it was so small. The vision then panned to the next day. It again showed me walking up to that same porch area. I again see this hole and now it is about 6" wide. I see that it is growing wider. I quickly look at it and I feel that maybe a dog or gopher made it.

As the vision continued on the third day, it showed me walking up to the porch area. I notice that hole, but now it is about three feet wide! Concerned, I go over to look at it and I cannot see a bottom to it. Now I feel a bit scared. I am now thinking whether this hole is going to get so big it will suck in our home. I now get the idea that I have to fill it in to stop it growing. I get a shovel and start to fill it in from dirt from my property.

It seemed to take hours as the hole appears bottomless. Finally, I filled in the hole to the top and patted it down with my shovel. Almost immediately, the dirt in the hole starts to shake. Then out comes what looks like a little baby Eagle. It then walks around me in a circle. Then the dirt shakes again and out comes another baby Eagle and it joins the circle.

And then the dirt shakes even more and out comes what appears to be the much bigger Mother Eagle. She now joins the circle with her babies. Finally, the dirt was really rumbling when out comes the huge Father Eagle. All the Eagles then get in line and dance a circle around me and then walk down my walkway into the neighboring street. That's the end of the vision. What a vision! So precise and in the form of a movie.

Of course, I tell Caroline about this amazing vision later that morning. I cannot get it out of my head. That afternoon on a partly cloudy day, I was in my backyard and took lots of photographs of the clouds. I had no idea what cloud formations I would find in those photographs.

That evening I downloaded the new photographs and noticed one very strange one. As I looked closer, I noticed the image of an Eagle from the neck to the beak, including all of its head in a profile position. I was amazed at the eagle's curved beak, big eye, and closed mouth. It is shown flying upwards into the sky.

Now I wondered how his vision of the eagle that early morning had translated into a cloud with an eagle image? What did the vision mean? What is the meaning of the Eagle? Sometimes I consult my "Animal Spirit Guides" book by Steven D. Farmer for the answer.

When I looked at the meaning of Eagle in his book it stated, "It is a time of a great spiritual awakening, one where you experience a greater connection to the Divine." Little did I know how true that meaning would become over the next six years. The following year on 11-11-2011, I would be shown the meaning of Divine Love delivered by two Angels in human form. You will read that story about the Navajo vision and our trip to Monument Valley later in this book.

The New Baby in the Clouds As a Symbol of Rebirth

One afternoon on June 11, 2011, I was taking quite a few photographs. It was a mostly cloudy day. Yet, I seemed to be drawn to take them that day even though there was not much to see in those clouds. Given the cloudy day, I could have easily not taken any photographs.

While I did not see anything in particular, when I downloaded the photographs onto my computer that night I was astonished. I could not believe that I spotted a newborn baby's head and face in those clouds. It was a faint image, but it surely was there. I said to myself, "How could this happen?" "What did it mean?" "Was this another message from the Clouds?" The photograph shows the baby's face in the center of it. It shows the entire bald head, one eye, nose, and mouth.

Usually seeing a new baby would mean a new life or a new beginning. Perhaps a rebirth-like the Phoenix Rising. In looking back at my life at that time, a new beginning was certainly coming on December 21, 2012.

I have learned that if you keep an open mind to the Magic all around, you will see messages coming to you. Those messages can come in the form of animals, butterflies, or insects visiting you, or a person you don't know giving you advice, or even Angels in human form contacting you. Perhaps like this story, a message from the Clouds.

King Daniel Appears in the Sky

In 2009, I had spent long hours creating my first book called "Journey to the Clouds – Messages from the Sky." In June 2009, I was anxiously waiting for the copies of the book to be delivered to my house. I am sure that you can imagine how excited you might be to get the copies of your first book after spending so much time and effort creating it. Finally, I got the call that it was coming later in the day. I went home and waited for the truck to arrive.

While waiting, I decided to do some chores around the house and happened to go outside into the front yard. I looked up at the sun and saw this huge cloud over the sun. I ran into the house to get my camera and took several pictures of this very unusual cloud. Later, I looked at the photographs on my computer. I was clearly astounded by the photographs of that day.

My first impression of the cloud was that it was a being of royal nature, or a king, as it appeared to

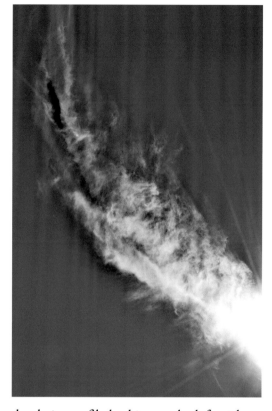

have something on its head. I could see the face very clearly in profile looking to the left with an outline of its head and face, nose, eye, and mouth...and its hands appeared to be clasped together as if in a praying position. I decided I needed some help deciphering these photos.

I emailed the photo to my psychic friend, Francie Marie, who has given me great advice over the years. She almost instantly replied that she was getting that this was a representation of King Daniel. I felt her answer was just unbelievable. How could this be? Why this sort of cloud over my house? What did it mean?

As you can imagine, I did some research on the internet about Daniel, the Book of Daniel, Daniel in the Bible, Daniel and the den of Lions, etc. He was regarded as a saint, prophet, and famous for interpreting dreams. Daniel was at the time of Ezekiel, King Cyrus the Great, and Babylon, and so much more. Could Francie Marie be right?

What is truly weird is that this cloud came the same day and moment of the delivery of my first book to my home. Did the cloud have something to do with my book coming that day? For me, I am going with Francie Marie's interpretation as there are no other logical explanations that I have found. Perhaps someday we will all know what this cloud means.

Francie Marie Predicts the STARGATE in France

Some say that psychics are fakes. Surely, some are. But some have incredible gifts as they connect with your Angels and Guides. Francie Marie is a very gifted psychic. She became one after years of training and practice.

Since 2007, I had several experiences where she predicted something for me or informed me about my life. One of the really stunning predictions she made was that Caroline and I would see a Stargate when we ventured into England and France in 2008. I had a psychic session with her a couple of months before our trip. During that session, she told me quite calmly that I would see a Stargate in France and that when that happens, it would be guarded by several Angels and I must honor it. She added that she did not know how it would be presented to me or what it would look like.

After I left that session, I felt like that was weird and would never happen. And why a Stargate? By the way, a Stargate is thought to be an opening where you could access another dimension besides our own or perhaps to travel great distances rapidly within our own dimension and universe.

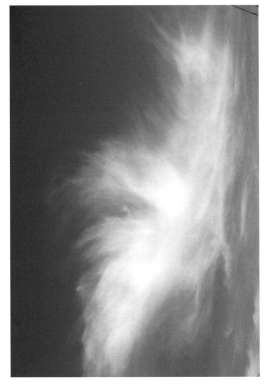

When we got to France, we took a train from Paris to the Brittany region in the northwest. As we arrived in a place called St. Malo, a beach town in France, clouds were forming overhead. There was one huge one that looked like it had a head and arms. We then took a taxi to the area of town which also abuts the huge beach. Caroline got out to get us a hotel room and I got out and surveyed the beach and downtown buildings.

Next I looked up and saw to my left some tiny clouds that looked like Angels. Then I looked straight up and saw this incredible humanoid-looking cloud that had legs, an arm, hand, and finger, and a head. It reminded me of that Predator Creature in the Predator movie. Its arm and finger were pointing downward. But why? [see photo on next page]

As I looked downward, I saw what that humanoid cloud was wanting me to see. It was this huge cloud with a triangular opening in its center.

It was stunning just to be there and absorb it. It felt so surreal, like time had stopped. I started to take photos of all these clouds as quickly as I could.

The cloud was uniquely positioned over the row of downtown buildings so I could really get a perspective about how big it was.

As I stood on the sidewalk taking these photos, I noticed that I was the only one looking at this cloud. About 40 people walked by me while I was taking these photographs.

I then noticed a cloud cluster to the right and took that one. It appeared that at least one cloud entity was looking in amusement at the whole event with his arms and hands supporting his head.

I think you know that when someone near you looks up, it makes you want to see what that person sees. Not only was I looking up, I was looking up with a large camera and huge telephoto lens. You could not miss that I was taking this cloud. But no one stopped, and no one looked up. I could not believe it! I continued to take photo after photo as I did not know when this would evaporate. I zoomed in! [see photo on opposite page]

As I processed what was happening, I knew in my heart that this was the Stargate that Francie Marie had predicted. It was so beautiful. Just stationary in the sky. It lasted a few minutes rather than quickly evaporating or changing. I felt inside of me that Time had stopped! I don't know why but it felt like I was an observer of something awesome. As Francie Marie directed, I stopped taking photos and honored the Angels and the Stargate.

By the time this event was over, Caroline had gotten us a room in the hotel across the street. I told her she missed the event of the century! I was fortunate that I captured it all on my camera to show her later.

What a trip to England and France! We had lots of fun and discovery in both countries. The real treat was being right there with that Stargate in the sky. I was smart enough to have my camera with me to be able to document this event and share it with everyone.

Merlin Pays a Visit

One day in 2013 I was out in my backyard looking at clouds over my house and all of a sudden some clouds started to swirl like a tornado. These gray and white clouds started creating what looked like a vortex. Then it got faster and faster. It seemed to be getting closer and closer to me. It was so huge that I started to be a little scared to be honest about it.

It seemed to transform into different images. Then it ended with an incredible image. It appeared to be an image of an older man, with squinty eyes, wrinkled forehead, and long white beard. Then I got a strong message in my head. The message is that this was not an ordinary old man... it was Merlin himself. Known as a wizard for his magic and superpowers, Merlin dates back centuries in England. Without a doubt, this transformation of clouds was a very special event.

 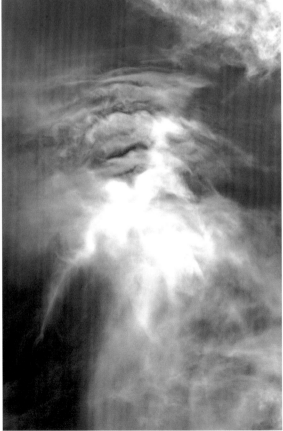

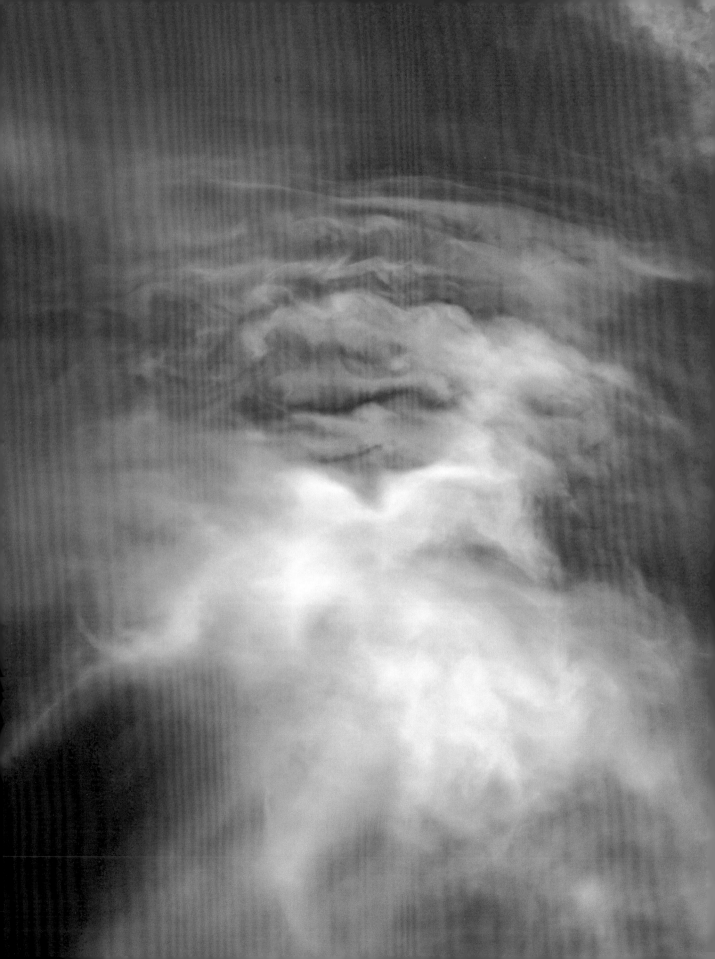

Francie Marie Leads Us to the Hawaiian God Cloud on the Big Island of Hawaii

In September 2008, Caroline and I went to the Big Island of Hawaii for a vacation. Before we left, I had a visit with my psychic friend Francie Marie. Almost immediately, she said her guides were telling her that I needed to go to where the lava meets the ocean on the Big Island. She added that I needed to see the clouds of water vapor there which will swirl like a tornado. I knew that Francie Marie had been right so many times in her predictions that I better do as she says.

When we arrived on the Big Island, we definitely made a trip to where this lava was flowing out and hitting the ocean. This area is full of ancient lava flows that have hardened.

As we got closer to where the lava flows into the ocean, the hot lava created mountains of steam. A steam cloud if you will. I noticed that the steam cloud was now changing from an amorphous mass into a spiral like a tornado. It was not the typical shapeless cloud of steam. At that moment, I told Caroline that Francie Marie was right...it is in a spiral motion.

As we watched the spiral steam cloud, we could see what looked like a little body and arm. I kept taking pictures of it and then all of a sudden, this incredible steam cloud formed into a discernible image of a huge human with a large head, eye, bent nose, mouth, part of a shoulder, and a large rounded belly. It was simply amazing to see this rapid transformation of the steam into a visible Being of some sort.

When we got back to California and looked at our photographs of it, both of us felt that it was something so very special and powerful. To us, it looked like an ancient ruler or King. Or a God! Could it have been the image of an ancient ruler on Hawaii? We named it "The Hawaiian God!"

Perhaps we will never know the precise message. Clearly something wanted to create this for us to see. Otherwise, Francie Marie would not have gotten the psyhic message. The question is what forces are at work that give an advance warning to Francie Marie of a future event such as this.

I think the message is about the Magic in the world. How best to demonstrate it to us than through such an amazing image...a creation of something Godly! They wanted us to witness it and to tell others about it. So we have, haven't we?

The Divine Feminine Presence in the Sky

On one very cloudy afternoon, I took some cloud photographs for fun. It was an exercise in frustration as the sky was completely gray. However, when I looked straight up, I saw a little more light coming through, but still no blue sky or hardly any definition of the cloud formations.

I decided to take a few photographs of that lighter area. There was a bit of color to that area of the sky as light tends to diffuse and refract to create rainbow-like colors.

Once I noticed these colored clouds I said to myself..."What the heck...Who knows if there is something there or not!" So I took several photos. Later, when I downloaded my photographs on my computer, I came upon the colored ones. I was absolutely stunned!

What appeared was an image of a female human-like being with long legs, one long arm, chest area with breasts, and a human type head...all with some coloration. Or was this human at all? In looking at the face of this image, I felt it was human-looking, but not human.

Why was this in the sky? Was there a message to this being presented to me? Nonetheless, on a very cloudy day, messages from the clouds were still being presented .

In thinking about this, I remembered that there was a lot of discussion in spiritual circles that the December 21, 2012 powerful energies that came into our planet were a beginning of a new era of feminine energy. Some believe that these energies are designed to create more of a balance of the Divine Masculine and the Divine Feminine Energies. Not surprising to me is the fact that this photograph was taken in 2012!

Perhaps the presentation of the Divine Feminine Cloud image in the sky overhead was a symbolic message of this energy coming into our Earth and the changes that many occur.

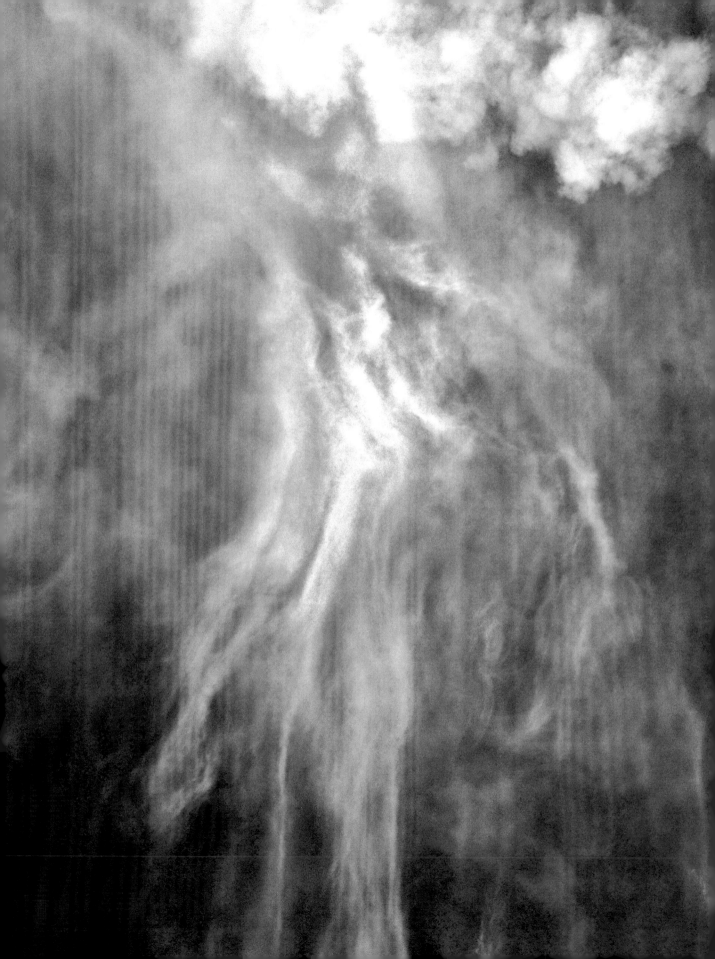

Joy

Chapter 5

Life Abounds on Earth

God not only plays dice, but he sometimes throws them
where they cannot be seen.
- Stephen Hawking

We seem to be discovering more and more different and previously unknown forms of life all the time. I remember reading a news article a few years ago where microbe life was found miles under the Earth's surface when a drilling company probed that deep. Imagine life that deep in the Earth where there is no light...only the heat of the soil, minerals and maybe some moisture. I also remember seeing videos of the latest discovery of life deep in our oceans some of which only survive near volcanic vents.

All of the theories of how and where life could exist on this planet have been shattered. Caroline and I were educated to believe that life had to have sunlight, water, oxygen, a food source, and so on. Those theories no longer work given the forms of life humans have discovered.

These are examples of life that are unseen until they are exposed or discovered. In this chapter, Caroline and I have found some life in the most unlikely places, and we have photographed it for you to see.

We Are Not Alone on This Planet

During our many adventures over the last 16 years, Caroline and I were surprised to find that there are many other life forms that live on our planet that normally humans cannot see. I explained earlier that I saw a Fairy approach me as I was sitting down in my backyard. That is the kind of life form I am referring to.

For example, Caroline and I travelled to the Big Island in Hawaii and arrived at the Mauna Kea mountaintop where the giant telescopes are located. I threw a white crystal down a steep slope and it rolled about 25 feet and stopped. I took a photograph of it and then another. I did not see anything unusual with my eyes.

When we got back home, I looked at those photographs on my computer. One was normal and the other had a pair of orange beings of some sort near the crystal. After research, I found out that they were very likely to be the sacred Menehune people. It appears that the Menehune in the photograph were interested in the crystal and therefore went to it for a brief second.

In Hawaiian mythology, the Menehune are beings who live on the mountains of Hawaii. They are said to be short in height and orange in color, just like our photograph shows. The Hawaiian native peoples honor them and try to protect them from human interference on the mountains.

Another example is our discovery in the San Francisco Mountains of Arizona in the Flagstaff region. Caroline and I went near the top of one of the mountains at 9,000 feet. We walked about 45 minutes into the forest and then Caroline asked me to stop and rest. She sat on an old log and then told me to take a photograph of the small pine tree next to me. I asked her why that one since there are so many pine trees around me. She said she felt it was important. So I took photographs all around the area that we were in and of that pine tree.

When we got home to see our photographs, there was a translucent white mass moving from the trees closer to Caroline and then it engulfed her. Another photograph showed that small pine and the trees behind it. We then noticed a translucent face above the small pine

looking at us from behind the larger tree in the background. This face reminded me of a clown face with the make-up. Its hair was orange and had whiskers like a cat. It seemed to be very interested in us.

I researched this kind of being and found out it may be a Wood Sprite. They live in forests around the world but we cannot see them. They are shy and probably frightened of us because we cut down their homes...the forests.

Then there are the entities that I have captured through my photographs of sidewalks. Somehow, these images sometimes pop up on sidewalks perhaps as communication to us. For example, there is the large one that I found when I was jogging one day. I had to stop as soon as I noticed it. It was dark brown and had the appearance of a woman with long hair. It had one eye showing and a nose and lips. Interestingly, it showed its feet in typical women's pointed shoes. I went back the next day and it was gone. Was it just a fleeting message for someone that happens upon it or was it for me?

Another day while jogging, I happened upon another sidewalk image. It seemed to be a bull or cow in a standing position looking to the left, and it is back to back with a human male who seems to be standing as well.

One time when in Oahu, Hawaii, Caroline and I took a walk around Honolulu. We were walking on the sidewalks in the different neighborhoods when I noticed a very clear image of a woman's face in the sidewalk. The image appears to show her eyes and mouth and her hair was up or she had a crown of some sort.

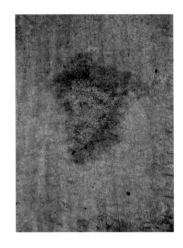

Caroline and I went on a sacred tour of Archangel Michael energies in the Canadian Rockies region. On our trip, I noticed several mountains that seemed to have faces. I snapped their pictures. When we came home, our photographs revealed "real" faces in those mountains. For example there is the one face that looks like a mountain face of a man with eyes, nose and mouth.

Then there is the other male looking face in the mountain that has one eye, a nose, and mouth, but there is a horizontal rectangular strip under its eye. That strip looks like a rectangular band aid.

But when that area is magnified a little, it reveals faces of what looks like people. Especially the one in the middle!

We were able to photograph another mountain in the Canadian Rockies that just looked so beautiful with the clouds overhead. Again, when I put the photograph on my computer, I turned it on its side and it revealed a face of what looks like an animal like some sort of cattle with its eye, longer  snout, and mouth. But what is interesting, this face is looking directly at a cloud face. Were these two magical beings talking?

Many people believe in ETs, Extraterrestrial Beings, or Alien life forms. Caroline and I believe that alien life has been here from long ago and perhaps such life is here now. In 2008, Caroline and I went to Egypt on a tour of the country. One day we arrived at our hotel in Cairo and our tour group got together for dinner.

I went over to another table where some of our group was sitting to say "hi" to one of the people. The woman who I approached turned her head to look at me and her face turned completely into a Lizard appearance. Her face reminded me of an alligator or lizard. I have studied the alien phenomena since I was a child and one of the theories is that a race of intelligent reptiles called Reptilians or Draconians are among us on the Earth. The theory is that they can shapeshift from a Reptilian appearance to that of a human being. It is possible, according to some people, that these Reptilians are in camouflage so that they can walk among us without being noticed. Some believe that their agenda is not to help us. I have to say seeing this woman transform was unbelievable and scary, so I left immediately.

While I don't have a photograph of the Reptilian, I do have some interesting pictures of clues to an alien race coming to the Earth. While Caroline and I were in Sedona, Arizona in 2008, we found a museum that was named the Ringing Rocks Foundation which exhibited Shaman from around the world. These are powerful spiritual leaders of our world. One of the exhibits was of Vusamazulu Credo Mutwa from South Africa.

The story goes that he visited a place deep in Africa that had a tribe of people that looked very human except that their feet were hooves like a horse. The ancient legend of this tribe is that they came from the star system of Sirius long ago. The tribe is called the Bantwana for "Children of the Stars." The exhibit showed Vusamazulu Credo Mutwa in his shaman clothing with a huge necklace. I noticed the images on his necklace and saw what appeared to be a flying saucer with the landing legs and ladder. Of course, Caroline and I were amazed at what we saw.

We were amazed because we had seen that image the day before on our jeep tour of Sedona. Our guide "Storm" took us at our request to visit any petroglyphs that were of an alien type. She said she had seen some and then took us south of Sedona in a mountainous area. We climbed along a shallow cliff face to discover an ancient petroglyph image that was virtually identical to the one seen on the shaman's necklace. Now the question you have to ask yourself is how could the flying saucer image on the shaman's necklace from Africa be the same image as seen engraved in an ancient petroglyph a half a world away in Sedona, Arizona? Both of these images are likely thousands of years old.

Yes, in our view, there is no question that many other forms of life exist on our planet that we cannot easily see. It is likely that legends and folklore have developed over the centuries as the people of those times experienced these life forms, including aliens from other than our planet. So interesting to think about, isn't it!

Extraterrestrials and My Buddha Statue

One day my friend Kathleen asked if I wanted her large concrete, but heavy, outdoor Buddha Statue. She was moving and it was so heavy she wanted to see if anyone would take it off her hands. Instantly, I agreed to take it. Soon I took the statue and put it in my backyard. It was perfect there.

Well, sometimes one person leads to another. I showed a photograph of this Buddha Statue to my friend Francie Marie. She quickly said to me that she was getting a message that I needed to take photographs of the Buddha that night. She added that "THEY" wanted to show me something. I asked who "THEY" was? She responded... "ET — the Extraterrestrials! They want you to know that they exist."

You know that most of us have a hard time believing in Alien life from outside our planet. We all want proof.

As usual, I follow messages and guidance. That night I took some photographs of the statue. I could not see anything unusual with my eyes. But when I loaded those photographs on my computer, it was clear that Francie Marie was right.

Amazingly, the Buddha Statue photograph now showed a fuzzy light coming off of it. That light is flowing upward and then that light combines into a ball of light. Then that ball of light transforms into a brilliant line or stream of light that travels into the sky. In one quick click of my camera, the photograph showed all of that – a fuzzy light, to a ball of light, to a thick stream of bright light.

I was convinced that this was so incredible. So many different forms of light in one click of the camera! Those could not be explained as natural reflections of light or anything else we consider normal.

That photograph is the proof that Francie Marie was right. I believe she was delivering the message of the Extraterrestrials. They want us to know that they are here among us.

Love and Peace

Chapter 6

Love and Peace Are Within Each of Us

When the power of Love overcomes the Love of power,
the world will know Peace.

— *Jimi Hendrix*

Love is the pure essence of our very being. It is the breath of life.
It is what binds us together.
To Love is to survive, to create,
and to hold one another in golden arms of peace.
It is our greatest ability,
our greatest gift, and it is that which will never escape us
as the powerful spirits we are."

— *Anonymous*

The following stories are about the guidance Caroline and I received along the way of finding genuine Love and Peace in our lives. We hope these stories enlighten you, inspire you, and give you hope that Love and Peace are attainable in all facets of your life. It is our belief that Love and Peace can spread around the world and overcome the greed, jealousy, and violence that exists. It just takes belief, motivation, and action. The first step is to simply hug someone each day.

Make Peace Within Yourself – Inner Peace

Many of us pray to the angels for Peace on Earth. But it seems our human history is filled with conflict between people – within families, communities, between nations, and certainly between races, and religions. To Caroline and I, Peace is the essence of being in the state of the Angelic.

Why is it so hard to have Peace? Perhaps these conflicts arise over jealousy, as in the story of Cain and Abel, or perhaps over greed that shows within families when the "Will" is read. Perhaps it is over the profit motive in businesses and corporations. There are so many instances of it. Why is Peace so elusive? Peace perhaps scares people. Actually, none of us have ever lived in a world of Peace. Most of us really don't know what it is and don't know what it feels like. Many of us have not experienced Peace within ourselves or in our own families. If you read local papers or the internet news every day, there is no Peace. Instead we are brought the everyday list of killings, torture, drugs, rapes, sexual abuse, and conflicts on a global basis. That is not Peace. Often we feel helpless to change it.

We believe that the only way to effect a change towards worldwide Peace is on a personal basis. If we do not have "Inner Peace" or Peace within ourselves, how can we expect to have worldwide peace?

We believe the key to Inner Peace is to use the Heart to change yourself from within. With the Heart actuated so to speak, perhaps each of us could find a way to love ourselves first. With the Heart, perhaps each of us could remove the greed, jealousy, hatred, intolerance, and the large ego that may be within us. If so, these traits could be replaced with pure Love for ourselves and for others, and for our whole planet. Imagine a state of Love within each of us! A state of mind that would love instead of hate, that would be tolerant of all people, that would not place money above all other things, that giving was so much better than taking, and to believe that our egos could be tempered to allow others into our lives.

There is no quick solution for Peace. But imagine if you as one person could attain a state of Peace [and the Love that goes with it] within you, wouldn't that be enough? Imagine living each day in appreciation for all that you are and all that you have. Imagine helping others less fortunate because it is fulfilling. Imagine the thankfulness or gratitude you might have for just living on planet Earth, appreciating your sense of sight to see the colorful landscape or to peer into another's eyes, to wonder about the blue skies and white clouds, appreciating your sense of smell to breathe the scent of the air, your sense of touch to feel physical objects or even to hug another person, to let all your senses appreciate that river, sea, or ocean, to be able to "think," analyze, and imagine things with your incredible brain. But what is so amazing is that, you, as one person, have the ability to Love and Care and to share it with as many people, animals, insects, and plants as you wish. That is real Power! More power than any leader or corporate president because there is nothing anyone can do to stop or control you in your exercise of Love and Peace.

So you can have Peace on Earth! It is your personal Peace with yourself and all that you may choose to do in your lifetime. It is your expression of LOVE that allows you to have Inner Peace. These are the decisions that only you can make.

Caroline and I have chosen this path to the best of our abilities. We have reformed ourselves to appreciate all that we have and the world and people around us. The gift of this Earth is beyond words. Negativity in any form is not acceptable to us, and if we are confronted with it, we remove it. Each day is an opportunity for us to live a life of Love and Peace. We accept that opportunity as we get up each morning and realize how blessed we are. We wish you success in finding Love and Peace!

Meditation and Walking the Labyrinth

Many people wonder how they can find inner peace. Quiet solitude is needed in order to let the mind relax and open up to messages and guidance. This can be practiced in many ways. Even a few minutes a day can be very rewarding.

Journaling can be a form of meditation and a way to let your thoughts flow. Silent walking in nature is very pleasant and relaxing. Prayer or meditation in a special location in your home or yard can give you a break from the everyday chaos of modern life. Listening to quiet music or a fountain relaxes the mind.

We are fortunate to live by a large open space with trees, grasses, wildlife, birds, and a creek with several waterfalls. We are able to visit this area almost daily. We strive to quiet our minds and say a special mantra that has evolved over the past few years. It is a reminder and a message of love, peace, joy, protection, and patience which helps us each day to be committed to each other and to our path.

Through these forms of meditation we practice quieting the mind. Sitting in a quiet place might work for you also. It takes practice and patience. Try to make the place just for you with special stones, plants, photographs, and a comfortable cushion or chair.

Labyrinths have also been a way for us to quiet our minds and to reflect on our journey. We discovered the first labyrinth that we walked at the Grace Cathedral in San Francisco. There is both an indoor labyrinth which is open during church hours and an outside one that is open 24 hours a day.

The Reverend Dr. Lauren Artress founded Veriditas, an organization to promote the revival of the labyrinth as a tool of meditation. She describes labyrinths as "a spiritual tool that has many applications in various settings. It reduces stress, quiets the mind and opens the heart. It is a walking meditation, a path of prayer, and a blueprint where psyche meets Spirit."

Labyrinths have been used for hundreds of years. They all have a single path into the center and after pausing to express your gratitude or to say a prayer, you return on the reverse path to exit the labyrinth.

This form of meditation was used in ancient times in many cultures and again in Christian times. It is said that pilgrims who wanted to walk to the Holy Lands but could not make that long and difficult journey would instead walk, sometimes many miles, to a location in a church or other sacred place where there was a labyrinth. Chartres Cathedral in France, which we visited in 2014, was one of these places.

In recent years there has been a resurgence of interest in labyrinths and creating them. They have been created with cloth, paint on cement, stone, bricks, grass, rocks and even marble.

We have found them in churches, church courtyards, parking lots, grassy fields, lawns, cemeteries, wooded areas, and along a coastal bluff overlooking the ocean.

The history of each labyrinth tells a story of how people need a peaceful meditative place to reflect on life, quiet the mind and receive inner peace.

We have probably visited over 100 labyrinths around the world. Whenever we travel, we try to locate a labyrinth in the area using the World Wide Labyrinth Locator at Veriditas.org. We even built one in our backyard on a large 20 x 20 cement area that we had never really used. It was like it was waiting there for us to create our labyrinth. It is just peaceful to go out on a quiet morning and walk the labyrinth.

Sometimes we just happen upon a labyrinth when we are exploring a place. Recently a new labyrinth was created at the Episcopal Church in St. Helena, California. We had taken a walk in the older neighborhood of town and luckily found this lovely, peaceful spot.

We hope you have a chance to visit a labyrinth and feel the peacefulness of walking on your path. You can find out more about labyrinths and locate one near you by visiting Veriditas.org.

Life is the path you make. Walk your own way!

The Synchronicity of the Message of Peace

In 2008, Caroline and I went to England to tour the country. We visited London, Stonehenge, Glastonbury Tor, and other sacred places. While back in London, we made a point of seeing Battersea Park. You see, we had heard about the Peace Pagoda there.

As we approached the entrance, there was a sign that indicated the sorts of things to see in the park. Well, of course, number 11 of all numbers was the Peace Pagoda. I was born on 11/11/1948, so I always resonated with the number 11. Then after getting involved spiritually a few years ago, I found out that 11 was a sign of the Angels.

In addition, 11/11 resonated with me since November 11, 1918 at 11:00 in the morning was the date and time of the signing of the "Armistice of 11/11/1918" which stopped all fighting of World War I between the Allies and Germany. So seeing an 11 always felt to me to be a sign of something Angelic and Peaceful and a sign to watch for something to happen.

That was certainly true for this occasion. So we walked down the path to the Peace Pagoda. It was huge and so well done. Situated on top of a small hill, it commanded prominence. And it was peaceful and quiet there. It was surrounded with a large landscape of grass and shrubs and trees.

We spent at least an hour there investigating the four sides of the Pagoda and all the written information provided at the base of the structure. It was so beautiful with four golden Buddhas representing each phase of the Buddha's life and journey.

Within 15 minutes of leaving the park, we were walking the London public sidewalks. Now I have to say that Caroline identifies with a Raven in its many character traits. One of those traits is how the Raven is attracted to finding shiny objects and then flying off with them. Caroline is the same. She is always looking down and surveying the ground and sees objects I never see.

All of a sudden, she sees a very tiny shiny object on the sidewalk. We go over to look at it and cannot believe what we are seeing. Caroline picks it up and puts it in her palm. She has found a tiny Peace Dove charm that would fit on a bracelet!

What a weird discovery after just visiting the Peace Pagoda. You wonder why that particular Peace Dove charm was there on that sidewalk, rather than the multitude of charms likely on that bracelet.

Finding that Peace Dove sent shivers down our backs. We had just spent our afternoon absorbing the Peace Pagoda in the park. Then we were reminded that Peace is so important. We were reminded that we should have Peace in our hearts and that we should spread Peace. We were reminded that each individual should strive to have that inner Peace in how they would think and act.

Unfortunately, we all live in a world consumed by violence. Violence occurs every day throughout the world. We have a habit, as humans, of creating violence against each other in so many creative ways. Not to mention our violence against animals and our planet.

So finding this Peace Dove is a reminder of the world we are in, and to try to find Peace in any way you can.

You have to say that the odds of finding a small Peace Dove charm 15 minutes after visiting the Peace Pagoda have to be rather nil. It was a reminder through a synchronistic event that Peace is so important and should be a part of our lives.

Think about it….PEACE!

Open Your Heart and You Will See

Decades ago it was very common that you would say "Thank You" for a gift received, or a simple favor done. Or you would write a special note in your own handwriting and mail it expressing your feelings of appreciation. Unfortunately, you don't see that so much in today's world.

In 2013, I was awakened out of a sound sleep like someone threw water on my face. It was Archangel Michael waking me at precisely 6:00 a.m. I quickly sat up in bed and then the message came. It felt like he "typed" this message in my forehead.... "Send this book to all places named St. Michael!" I had just completed our third book "Simply Angelic – Divine Images."

I thought what was that about? I was startled but then I thought about the message. I realized it was the perfect message. The message was to send the book to people who are more likely to believe in Archangel Michael. They would be more likely to appreciate and understand what the book is about.

So I went on my computer and I started researching places named St. Michael in the U.S. and the world. The internet makes this exercise so much easier. For example, I discovered Great Britain has 687 such places. I also discovered similar places are all around the world. Such places that I found were churches and cathedrals, schools, and public buildings. But in order to do this, I had to do it "cold turkey" so to speak. In other words, I had to gift the book and also pay for the postage. All the costs would be paid by myself. I had to expect that nobody would return a check to me for this gift. It had to be "FREE."

So I started sending out three to four books each day starting that very day that Archangel Michael sent me that message. I included a two-page letter explaining why I was sending it to them. It was a lot of work to do this each day and get them to the post office. I would send them all over the world. The book had been costly to produce and print as it had 250 pages of color photographs. Postage to places like Europe, China, and Australia could be several times the cost of the book. I even sent copies to famous people like Pope Francis.

It was a wonderful exercise in giving of myself, but also in spreading the information I had gathered for people to digest. Hundreds of books were sent out. I still do it. It also got me to give out my books for free to people and organizations in my local area. For example, my chiropractor allowed me to put my free books on her lobby counter. At least 100 of them were taken over the course of two months.

A typical comment from people was "nobody does anything for free anymore." People are surprised when something is free and unconditionally gifted. I guess I proved them wrong! This exercise in giving can be frustrating when you don't receive any positive feedback. But that did not deter me in my fulfillment of Archangel Michael's request. I knew he had a reason for me to do this. I was surprised however at how many people would accept this gift from me and did not even say thank you, email me or write me a note of thanks. Especially since sending a quick email could take less than five minutes.

We still have a few friends who practice the art of "thank you." One of our friends is a wonderful young woman named April. I have known her for many years and she would always find a way to thank you...by a card, or email, or a phone call. Always without exception! Sometimes she writes a note and mails it and also emails us expressing thanks. She is a shining light in the sea of people that don't care or who say they are "too busy."

Recently, Caroline and I took a tour to another country where we met a lot of people over several days. I would take their names and addresses and send them a copy of our book if they desired it. All at my expense, of course. Out of about 50 books that I sent out to these people, I only received a "thank you" from about 20. Sadly, this is typical in my experience. Then came the most wonderful "thank you" a few months after I sent out those books. It came from one of those

people – a woman named Tuli. We did wonder why it took her so long, but we appreciated her effort and her thank you. We emailed her letting her know that we had gotten the package she sent us including a "thank you" card inside. She was expressing her love and gratitude for our book as an inspiration for her spiritual journey. You could just feel that she spent a good deal of time and effort in this special gift back to us. She had sent us a beautiful hand-made ceramic heart with a matching key that could be attached to the back of the heart to symbolically unlock the heart. The message on the Heart was "KEEP A SONG IN YOUR HEART"!

In her reply to our email, she shared her story of this Heart. She described that our unconditional gift touched her so deep that she wanted to send us a meaningful thank you gift, but without knowing us she asked to be guided to that special gift for us. It was not the first item she picked. She bought something else first, but once she had it at home her intuition was telling her that this was not the special gift she wanted to get for us. Time went by and the holidays were approaching, so she was still keeping an eye open for that special thank you gift. After not finding anything, she decided to go back to the shop to return the gift she had already purchased. She said it was a very small local shop, so they don't carry that much inventory, nor do a lot of new items arrive frequently. However, she looked around one last time and there it was. It was that ceramic Heart that had just arrived with the lyric...KEEP A SONG IN YOUR HEART. She described that she had such a strong connection and knew immediately that was the gift she asked for.

In my email to her, I mentioned that the Heart with the song reference was very meaningful since my Dad was a musician who played the trumpet. Music was his life and it still is a part of our communication. I know from all my spiritual experiences that Angels communicate through art and music, so I felt this gift was a message from Above. Perhaps Tuli was guided by my Dad to select this Heart, a gift that was an expression of gratitude, love, and music. I am never surprised at my Dad and how he gives me messages directly or through others. Perhaps my Dad wanted to send a message to her and to us to never forget that we are constantly guided and loved. Love is so very important and should be incorporated into our everyday lives. Music is a great way to express it. Through this experience, she got a loving reminder of the power of Love. Her guidance and the perfect synchronicities that the Universe designs deliver such outcomes that are more fantastic than we can imagine.

I am firmly convinced that Dad was involved. He has been creating messages for Caroline and I to see and experience since 2011. All kinds of messages! He is always showing us that he is around us and is helping to guide us in the right direction. In this particular situation, he actually was helping Tuli who lived hundreds of miles away to decide the appropriate gift that would express her love and touch us in a profound way. That gift was more than a physical object. It was a gift that sent her gratitude to us in a way that her loving energy in turn filled our entire bodies when we received it. Caroline and I both felt it and we will never forget her gift and her.

I guess we should never be surprised about the impact of our decisions if they are based on unconditional love, giving and compassion. This story made me reflect more on the gifts of our book to those other people we did not receive a "thank you." I know that our unexpected gift to them made an impact on them even in a small way. Because of our book they may look to the skies and feel inspired, get mesmerized by the same beautiful clouds like the ones pictured in our book and ponder about their own connection to Above. In essence, they are looking for what we are all looking for each day...reminders of our True Self and manifestations of Love.

One of the things that makes us evolved humans is our ability to express, feel, and send Love. We are the Divine Caretakers and should care and love others, animals, insects, even rocks and our whole planet. We should Love and respect all of Divine Creation, the sky and clouds, oceans, lakes and rivers, the mountains and valleys, and all the life that abounds on our planet. We erroneously have taken those for granted in the way we live, we consume, we behave and disregard their presence and fragility, forgetting that we all have the right to live and thrive on this beautiful planet. Living busy lives has become the excuse to go through the motions of existence without imparting self-awareness and aliveness to our moments. Life becomes a series of repetitive motions without aliveness. No wonder the current state of affairs in the world. To us, everything starts from within each of us.

Imagine societies and businesses that incorporated care and Love in their daily decision-making. Imagine governments that worked with those principles imbedded in their daily operations rather than rely in false power egocentric structures and bureaucratic routes. Many times, gestures of the Divine come from someone that has the courage to take the time to pause, feel the Love and inner guidance around, and the awareness to impart aliveness to each moment by expressing love and appreciation.

We know through our spiritual experiences that the meaning of life on Earth for each of us is to Love and to express it in all ways possible. Our world would be so different if we all were able to manifest Love every day, reflect in our decisions, and how we live. Perhaps this story is an inspiration to you to ponder a little more about your own connection to the Divine, your guidance, your moment by moment awareness, and how you express and manifest Love to everything and everyone around you.

Open your Heart and you will see!

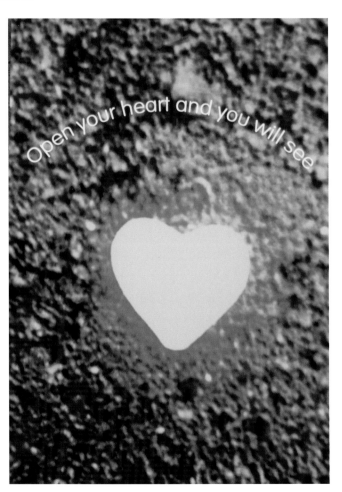

Lead with Your Heart

Caroline and I believe that the HEART and LOVE are so important to us as human beings and to our Souls. The Hearts are in this book because they are the essence of being Angelic.

Magically, the first Heart came after the Stargate cloud appeared in 2008 at St. Malo, France. The Heart was created by two sandworms coming together on the beach. We considered it to be a special message just after seeing the Stargate.

Magic was at work when the other heart came to us. As we took our daily walk, we found it on a nearby asphalt parking lot. It was a glowing bright red stone that you could not miss. What was so important is that it was so brightly glowing like it was entirely lit from within. We couldn't help but stop and take that picture and take that Heart home with us.

Both of these Hearts are so representative of the loving Magic that is all around us if we look and appreciate it. They remind us of the importance of our Heart and the Love that can come from it.

As our adventure has evolved since 2001, one of the most important lessons we have learned is how important the HEART and LOVE are for us as a species on this planet. We are heart-centered creatures. As such, the heart becomes the most important part of us.

Much has been written through history about the Heart and what it means. We take our Heart for granted, unless it causes us problems often as we get older. The Heart is more than just an organ pumping blood, which is certainly important.

But the heart is everything within us – it is our Soul, it is our meaning, and what we are on this planet. It is about the Love we have within us. It is the meaning of life. Especially, if we can embrace such things as Divine Love – the Love of all things created whether ugly or beautiful, big or small, black or white, whatever – it doesn't matter – LOVE FOR EVERYTHING THAT HAS BEEN CREATED.

We would like to convey the importance of – the Heart. Some of us really act and make decisions with our Heart. Many of us probably do not – and thus make decisions entirely from the brain. This is a huge distinction.

Here are some examples. If you acted from the Heart, you might act differently during an argument, since your Heart would make sure that you don't say something so terrible that you might regret later. You know, those words that are stored in your brain and you never should use against anyone. But in the heat of the moment, they come out. When they are out, the person you are talking to will never be able to truly forgive those words or forget them being used. By using the Heart, the Heart would prevent the brain from using them. In many ways, the Heart is so much smarter than the brain.

If you owned a business, and you had to lay off some employees, would you lay them off just before Christmas, or wait until a better time? The Heart would wait, of course.

If you had so much money that you could not use it all nor could your family – would you use that money just to keep for yourself and family, or use some of it to help others that are in more need? The Heart compels you to be in service to those in need.

If you encountered a "homeless person" laying on the sidewalk, would you walk by in disgust or just turn your head away? Or give that person some money to help him or her at that moment? The Heart would direct you to help in some way.

If you are thinking of doing something you knew would physically or emotionally hurt someone, would you go through with it or decide to stop it before it could do the damage? Of course, your Heart would make you reconsider.

My Mom and Dad were wonderful parents and I loved them so much while they were here on Earth. But they had a difficult time expressing their love in a physical way. I think the reasons for that are that they grew up in the hard times of the Great Depression and were just trying to survive, and also their families did not show love in a physical manner. A few years before their passing, I got the idea to hug each of them every time I saw them. That would be at least one or two times a week. Hugging was not something they did so when I started hugging them, they were so surprised. After a few hugs, they were hugging me back with great emotion. Such a little thing isn't it, but it shows the power of the Heart through physical actions. What a difference it made in our relationship over the remaining years with them! Even though I was not taught to hug, I love it and I do it with everyone I meet.

The list is endless with situations such as those above. Each day we are faced with decisions that challenge our brain and our Heart. Each of us can make a difference.

The Surprise Gift of Divine Love at Monument Valley

Since 2009, Caroline and I took care of my parents. They were quite ill and eventually both of them passed in the summer of 2011. Earlier in 2011, I had gone to a doctor's office with my Mom and noticed a magazine in the lobby that showed the new hotel in the Monument Valley Navajo lands located in northern Arizona. It looked so amazing. You may know this area of the Navajo lands. It was the setting of many Western movies with its beautiful desert scenery. I thought maybe one day we would be able to plan a trip to go there.

After my Mom passed in September 2011, I asked Caroline if we could go to the Navajo lands for a week and enjoy the hotel, the desert landscape, and try to heal from all the death that year. Caroline said she felt really concerned that winter was approaching and that we might get involved with too much snow in the area. She asked me to consider postponing it to 2012. I was disappointed, but I agreed.

So instead we decided to go to San Francisco and see the San Francisco Giants baseball game at the end of September. Earlier that day of the Giants game, we met our good friend Alan in San Francisco. We met Alan in 2009 and found that he is very spiritual and intuitive. He actually channels the "Beings from Above" you might say. As the three of us were having lunch together, I told Alan the story of going to Monument Valley and how Caroline wanted to postpone it to 2012. Almost instantly, Alan grows silent, raises his head a bit, and then says the Elders want to talk. He started to "channel." He said, "THE ELDERS ARE SAYING YOU MUST GO TO THE NAVAJO LANDS NOW!"

We were so surprised at how firm the message was from the Elders. Knowing Alan's abilities so well, Caroline knew that he was probably right. We were convinced. She then agreed to go as soon as we could arrange it.

Two weeks before we left, we took a long walk around our neighborhood. As we approached our home, a large cloud started swirling in front of our eyes. We wondered what was going on. All of a sudden the cloud manifested into this incredible and clear Native American Indian face – perhaps that of the Navajo Indian. It was so precise with the clear blue background of the sky. It was so surreal to see this cloud transform.

At that moment, we were glued to the cloud image and then we turned to each other and said simultaneously... "This is CONFIRMATION...absolute confirmation that we are supposed to go to Monument Valley!"

But we really had no idea why we were going other than to see the scenery and relax.

Caroline set up the visit for the second week of November – landing on my birthday of November 11th which turned out to be 11-11-2011. Caroline and I spent several days there and had a wonderful time. But we kept asking ourselves why are we here?

The last night of our trip, during dinner at our Monument Valley hotel called "The View," we sat next to two women from Philadephia. The mother was 92 and her daughter was in her 60s. The 92-year-old did all the talking and she was simply brilliant. We were so amazed that she spoke so eloquently. Our two tables were so close

we talked to each other quite a bit. I felt there was something different, even mystical about them. After dinner, we said goodbye to each other. We never thought we would see them again.

On the next morning, which was November 11, we started back to Phoenix in our rental car. We were planning a stop in Sedona, Arizona. Our trip was a four-hour drive from Monument Valley. We decided to see if our friend Storm was home in Sedona. She was, so we spent the afternoon with her touring Sedona. At 5 p.m., we decided to have dinner and found a place far out of the main town called Picasso's Pizza. It was crowded even at 5 p.m. We were able to get one of the last two tables left inside.

We just got comfortable in our seats, when we noticed a line forming at the door by people wanting to be seated. Then guess who comes in the door? Yes, those two women from Philadelphia came in and looked directly at us and smiled. Of course, we were so surprised at this chance meeting a day after our dinner together. It just did not seem possible.

Let's be frank here! It was impossible. First, we were four hours driving time from Monument Valley. Why did they also stop in Sedona? They did not know we were going to Sedona. They did not know we would go to Picasso's Pizza. They did not know we would be there precisely at 5 p.m.

I walked up to them and hugged each of them. The 92-year-old mother smiled and said to me that she had something important to tell me. She said to me that I must research something for her. I said of course I will. She then said very firmly "You must promise me!" I said I would surely do it whatever it was. She then said "You must research this...Julian of Norwich...promise me, Tom, that you will do this for me!" Of course, I said.

So Caroline and I had our dinner and said goodbye to the women. Later that night, I did some research on Julian of Norwich on my iPad. I found out that Julian was a young woman living in a church in Norwich, England in the 1300s. People were dying all around her due to the plague. And then she got sick as well. As she was dying of the plague, she told people around her that Jesus had come to her in 16 visions and spoke to her of many things. Jesus healed her and she lived into her 70s.

Julian later wrote several books based on the information that Jesus had passed on to her. The subject was DIVINE LOVE. Divine Love is a love for all of Creation, a Love for this planet we inhabit, a Love for all living things. Divine Love is a love for all that God Created...everything. And it is about Gratitude for all we have through this Creation.

I must say I generally understood Love. I also understood Unconditional Love. But I had not really thought much about Divine Love until that message from those two women. This message to us of Julian had now changed our lives. We had to reflect on it and incorporate it into our daily thoughts and actions. We had to change.

We also reflected on these two women. It is clear, without question, that they were sent to us to deliver this message. It is our strong feeling that these two women were not ordinary human beings. In our opinion, they were Angels in human form to deliver this message. A very important message of DIVINE LOVE!

Cheemah – Mother of the Spirit-Fire

During the last week of our preparation of this book, we seemed to have been guided perhaps by the Angels. We felt that we needed to go to Jack London Square in Oakland, California on our way to San Francisco. We had plans that night to see Burt Bacharach in concert in San Francisco.

Funny thing is that we had not been to Jack London Square for nearly 35 years. Why now? Well, we found out as soon as we got to the Square. In the midst of the Square was this very large sculpture. It was clearly of a woman and an eagle.

As we read the plaque, we found out that this was the image of Cheemah, the Mother of the Spirit-Fire. This sculpture was created by Osprey Orielle Lake. Osprey Orielle Lake is an artist and founder of the International Cheemah Monument Project. Her vision is to create eight such sculptures around the world to foster a bridge between cultures.

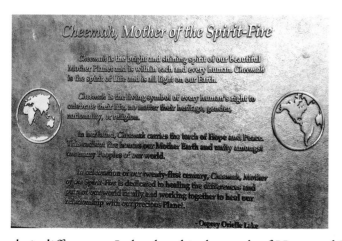

One of her goals with this sculpture was to inspire people to protect the Earth and all its wonders and beauty, and to help create a future where people can live in harmony with Nature and the Cities in a sustainable way.

In our opinion when we saw it, we were in awe of its beauty and its message. Its message was one of unity of the people of the world and healing of their differences. In her hand is the torch of Hope and Peace that suggests that we can all live in Harmony and Peace. Additionally, the sculpture honors Mother Earth and all its beauty and our role in protecting it.

When we understood what Cheemah was all about, it was clear to us that we were guided to see it, and to include it in our book as it complements our vision of spreading Love and Peace throughout the world.

You can read more about Cheemah and Osprey Orielle Lake at www.ospreyoriellelake.com

"Whoever Saves a Single Soul Saves the World in Time"

"Whoever Saves a Single Soul" is the title of a song on the "PEACE" album by Wayne Jones recorded in 2002. A few years ago, I heard it for the first time and I cried. I still get emotional every time I hear it. This song is about our human dilemma to help one another on this planet. It describes our calling to help each other. It is about loving each other and spreading that Love.

Similarly, our book is about our spiritual adventures which have led us to Love and Peace. Our adventures have a meaning...they are not just events. Their meaning, when all is said and done, is DIVINE LOVE and with that comes PEACE. Of course, Divine Love is the highest level of Love. Its meaning is Love all of God's Creations. That means all the other human beings on this planet, the animals, the plants and trees, the insects, and the entire Earth itself should be respected and loved by all of us.

So when Caroline and I heard it for the first time while riding in our car, we both felt "electricity" run through our bodies and we both cried. I really resonated with it. The words reflect the meaning of our book. The lyrics reflect upon how each of us has a Soul no matter what station in life we are in---for example, if we are in prison, or homeless living on the street, or whether we are filled with anger, or hate. The lyrics go on to say there is Love in each of us and that your Love can be spread to others that need help. The lyrics urge us to spread our Love and to help other Souls and in doing so, the world would be saved over time.

The words and the melody are so compelling and make you think of the things you can do to help others and to help yourself. To hear the song and see the lyrics, just research through the internet the "Peace" album by Wayne Jones and the last song on the album is "Whoever Saves a Single Soul Saves the World in Time."

Epilogue

There is a very special song that my Dad channeled through me one day during the preparation of this book. Perhaps he knew it had to be the Epilogue or ending of this book. It is called "Alfie" as written by Burt Bacharach and Hal David. The lyrics are beautiful and to the point that our existence is only really meaningful with Love. To hear the song and see the lyrics, research "Alfie" through the internet.

This song best captures the essence of our book, "The Magic of Finding Love and Peace". Life on Earth is about finding Love and the Peace within each of us.

We are so blessed to be able to share 16 years of our experiences finding Love and Peace. We hope you will think more about Love and Peace and what it means to you. We are sure there will be doubters, skeptics or pessimists that will not relate to this book. But what do they believe in? We say how can you be against Love and Peace?

We have shared with you the many stories that have shaped our beliefs and lives. These are actual and very personal events that are well documented with photographs. We believe that we are at a crucial time in Earth's history. Is my Dad correct in saying that some malevolent Aliens from a distant galaxy have discovered our planet and want to take it over, but that there are also benevolent Aliens trying to protect us? Is he correct in telling us that it is up to each of us to awaken, and to help our planet by visualizing our protective grid, or by saying a prayer for Earth with the hands of God around it.

It is our view that our lives are about Love…Love of ourselves, Love of others, Love of all life forms on our planet, Love of our planet in its entirety. With Love, all things can happen. With hate, jealousy, greed, and violence, there is only destruction of ourselves and our planet. The only sound and logical choice is to learn to Love and to practice it each day.

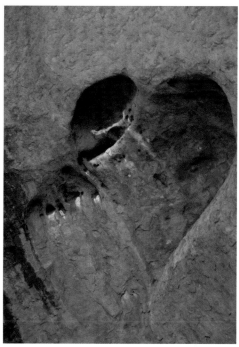

If we are fortunate in the precious years left in our lives, we plan to watch for messages and guidance each day and to continue our pursuit of Love and Peace.

Clouds and Meditations

Clouds that Remind Us of Angels

There is no doubt that clouds can look like our perceptions of Angels. We see them all the time, don't we? We are shocked with happiness if we are able to glimpse one such cloud, even for a brief moment. In our minds and our bodies, we feel the joy of having an Angel in our sight. They inspire us to think of the Afterlife, Heaven, the Goodness of Angels, and that perhaps an Angel is beside you protecting and guiding you. Please enjoy the following Angelic Clouds:

Meditation:

Respect for others comes from the heart.

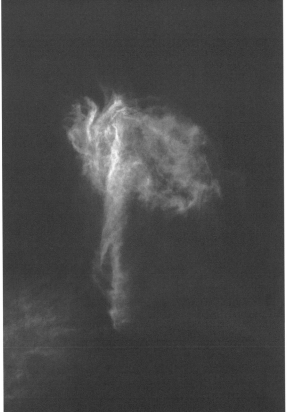

Meditation:

Music and dancing are perfect ways
to connect with the angels.

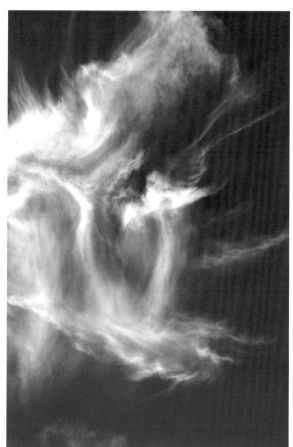

Meditation:

Spread love wherever you go

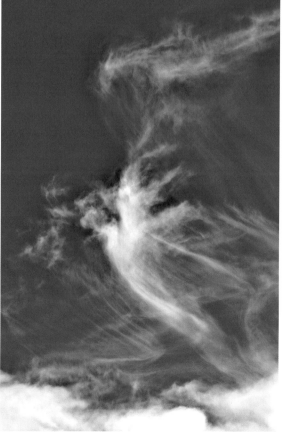

Meditation:

Freedom to choose your path.

Meditation:

Being strong is so important along the way of your path.

Meditation:

You have the choice to be angelic yourself.

Meditation:

Each day you can bring happiness to others.

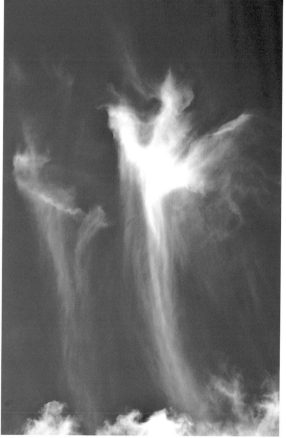

Meditation:

Courage is key to your spiritual growth.

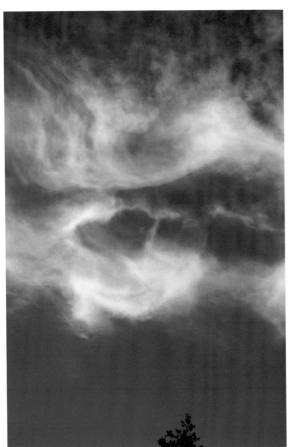

Meditation:

Open your heart and you will see.

Meditation:

Be still and quiet so that you can connect
with your angels and guides.

Meditation: Archangel Michael is always with you and protecting you.

Meditation: Divine love is the love of all creation.

Meditation: Never let fear make the wrong decisions for you.

Meditation: Life abounds all around you and honor it.

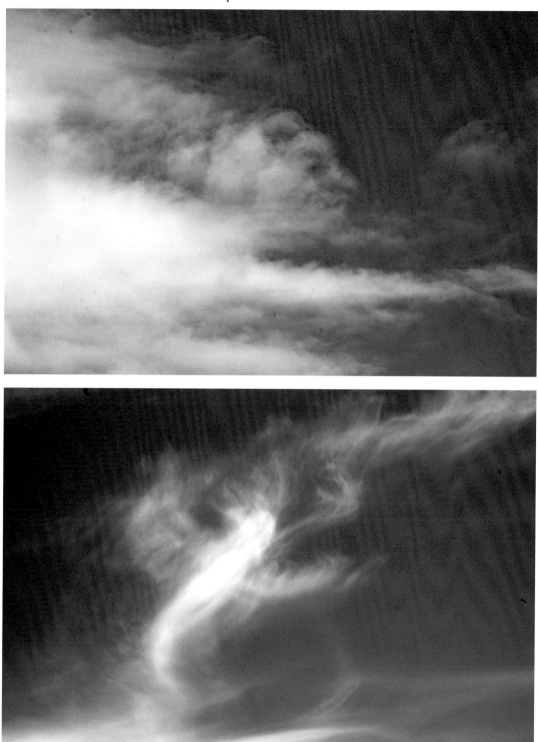

Meditation: Never give up on your spiritual journey.

Meditation: Kindness is an important aspect of your daily life.

Meditation: Your angel is coming to guide you if you will only open your heart.

Angelic Light of Healing

Clouds and Meditations

Clouds that Remind Us of Animals

Animals are all around us on our planet. Of course, we have our pets like the dogs, cats, aquariums of fish, exotic animals, and even the typical farm animal. Our Earth would be quite lonely without the animals that live alongside us. But then to see clouds that look like the animals we know, that is a real treat. It is always rewarding to see an animal cloud. That cloud warms our Heart. It is like someone painted that animal cloud in the sky just for us to see. Please enjoy these clouds in the images of animals:

Meditation:

Ponder the cloud above and ask if it is alive.

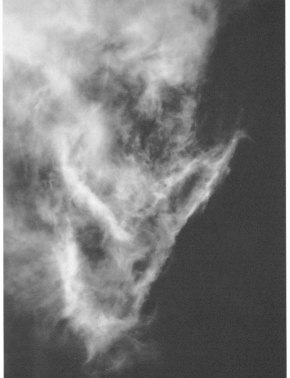

Meditation:

The Wind can sculpt the clouds
in so many ways.

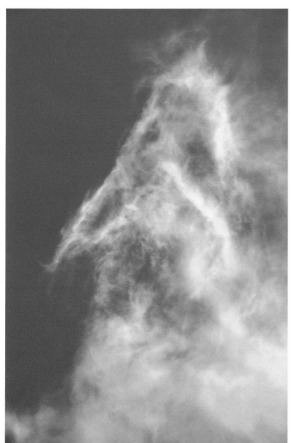

Meditation:

Wisdom can come from watching the sky.

Meditation:

Beauty is in all life forms on our planet.

Meditation:

You can look quiet and shy, but you know you are strong inside.

Meditation:

Have the patience of the cat.

Meditation:

Reach for the clouds and the heavens
to accomplish your goals.

Meditation:

Always survey the landscape around you
to make sure you are safe.

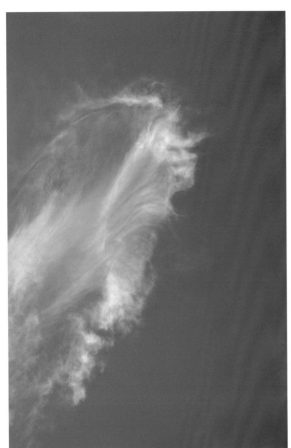

Meditation:

The courage of the lion can be yours as well.

Meditation:

Be persistent in all facets of your life.

Meditation:

Magical things can happen for you.

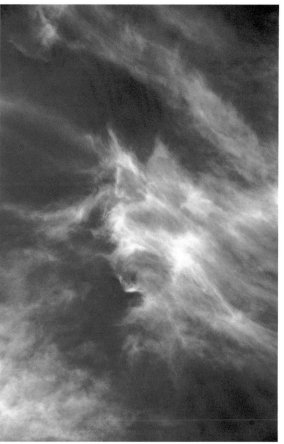

Meditation:

Perseverance is key to happiness.

Meditation: Show your strength when needed.

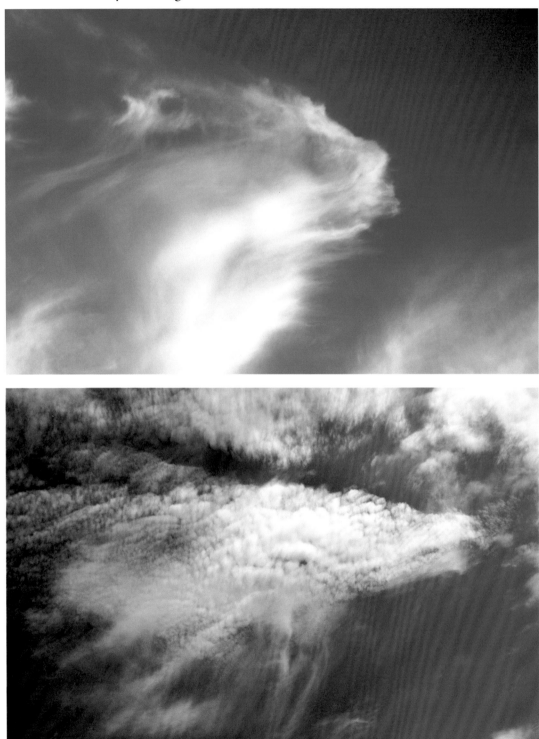

Meditation: Meditate like you have the patience of the whale.

Meditation: Let your mind fly with the angels into the heavens.

Meditation: Clouds can be many colors that make us feel alive and joyful.

Meditation: Be like the tiger and have no fear.

Meditation: Clouds can whisk by, but sometimes they are giving you a message.

Meditation: In your mind, meditate the image of a warm and sunny place that brings joy.

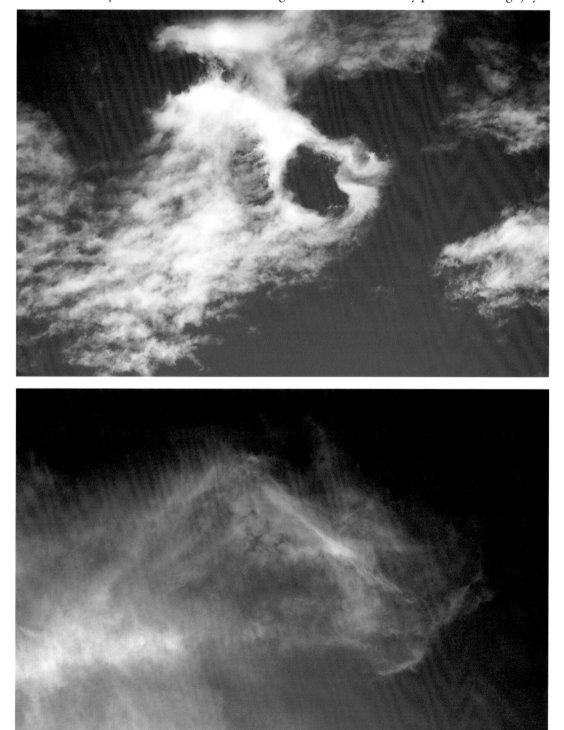

Meditation: It is time to free yourself of the confining aspects of your life.

Meditation: You may wish to plan an adventure to open your heart to love.

Meditation: Take advantage of opportunities that come your way.

Meditation: Make sure to spend time in solitude to energize your mind and body.

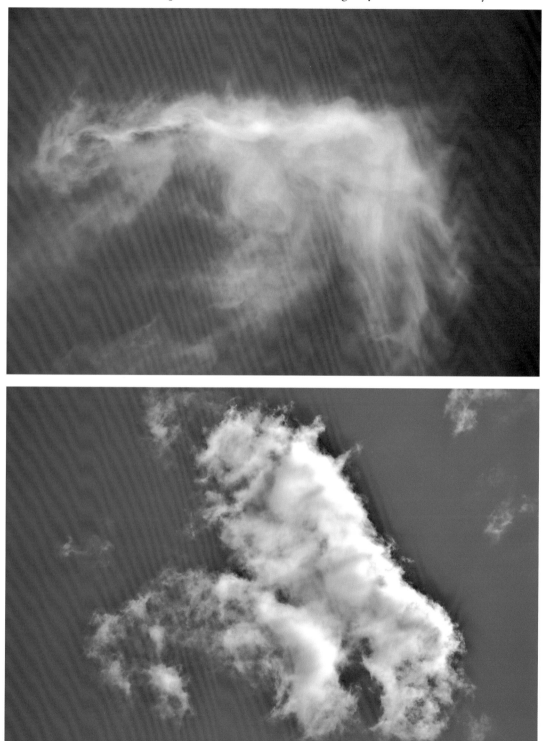

Meditation: Spend time with those who respect and love you.

Clouds and Meditations

The Orchestra of Clouds

When you think of an orchestra, you think of a group of people coming together to play their various musical instruments in harmony to create something beautiful to the ear. We call this "The Orchestra of Clouds" because it is the same thing, but in our sky in the form of clouds. Here we present to you a group of clouds perhaps the likes of which you have never seen. This group of clouds have come together to show you a variety of images in various types of cloud formations. You will see lots of happy and sad faces, an eagle with a man's face, a caterpillar, a magician, a man on a snowboard, someone reading a book, a man with a cigar in his mouth, a man sitting in a chair, and what appear to be many alien creatures.

We suggest you look for the head, eyes, nose, and mouth as you inspect each photograph. That will, perhaps, help you interpret the cloud image. Remember that what you see is your interpretation of the cloud. Another person might see another image that differs from yours. No one should criticize your interpretation just because they see something different. Both interpretations are valid. Please enjoy!

Meditation:

Always assess the landscape around you
so that you make the best decisions for you.

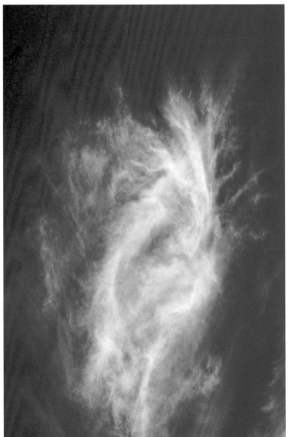

Meditation:

Be in a state of gratitude.

Meditation:

Be mindful of who you are.

Meditation:

Joy and happiness are within reach.

Meditation:

Be gentle no matter what size you are.

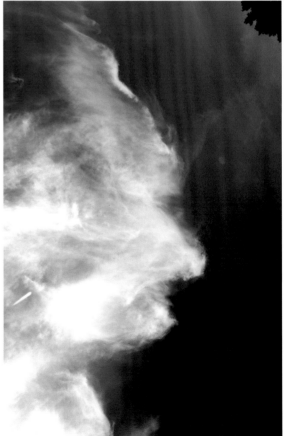

Meditation:

Don't interrupt others
when they are speaking to you.

Meditation:

Silence is so important in your life.

Meditation:

Have the courage to reach your goals,
no matter what anybody says.

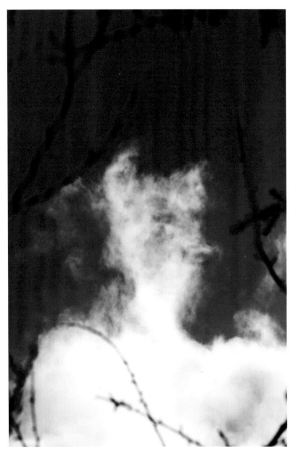

Meditation:

Don't hide from your true self.

Meditation:

Happiness is key to your success.

Meditation:

Sadness should be tempered with fun.

Meditation:

Don't stick your nose in other people's lives.

Meditation:

You are magic, so live like that.

Meditation:

Be confident in who you are.

Meditation:

Don't fly off – stay grounded.

Meditation:

There is an Angelic Book of the Principles
of Goodness and Love and Peace – follow it.

Meditation:

Honor yourself.

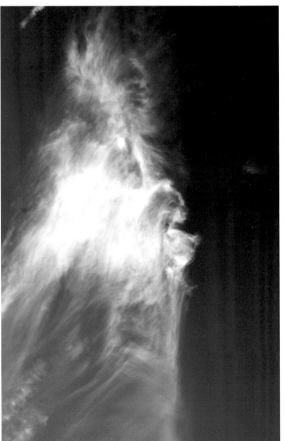

Meditation:

Even alien creatures love to laugh.

Meditation:

Be the light in someone's life.

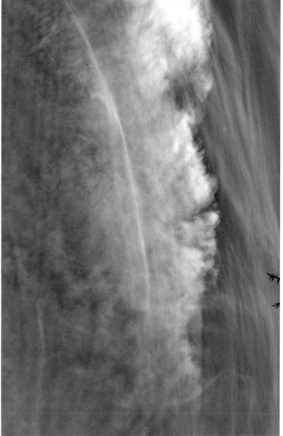

Meditation:

Wisdom should be a part of your life.

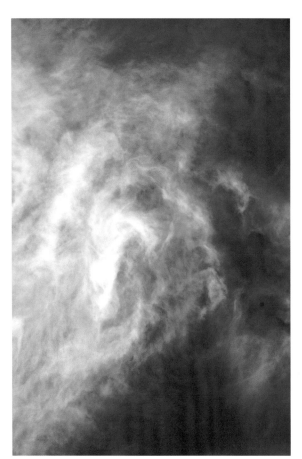

Meditation:

Look upward with hope and confidence.

Meditation:

It is important to listen
rather than talking all the time.

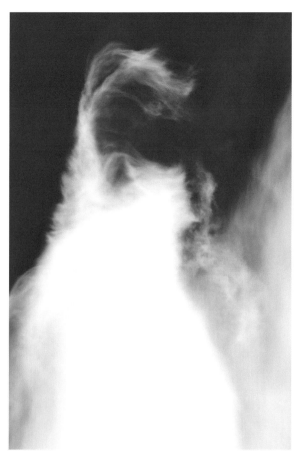

Meditation:

Be thankful for all you have.

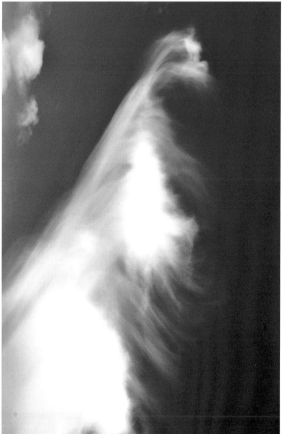

Meditation:

Have your antennae up and working
when seeking truth from lies — discern.

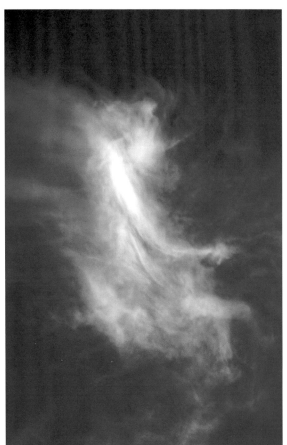

Meditation:

Be in the driver's seat of your life in every way.

Meditation:

Remember that you
are in charge of your life.

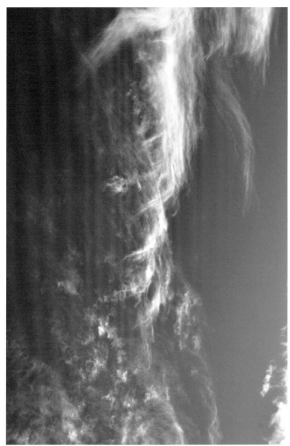

Meditation:

Sometimes it is better to be invisible and just watch others.

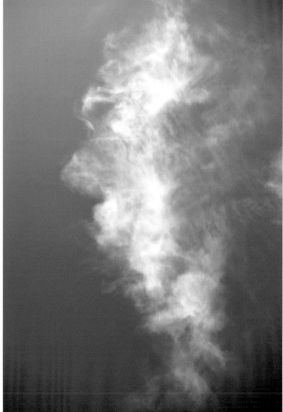

Meditation:

The cigar in your mouth does not make you special — think about it.

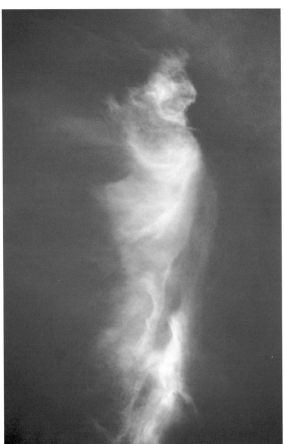

Meditation:

You may be different than others,
but that does not make you less of a person.

Meditation:

Always take advice gracefully
and then make your decisions.

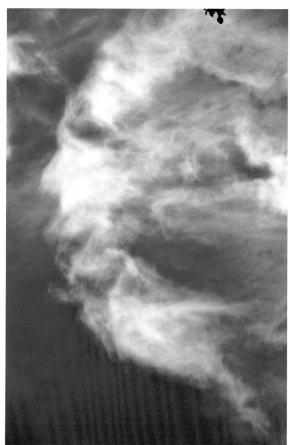

Meditation:

Remember that if you smile,
others around you will smile also.

Meditation:

You can give to others each day
if you only try.

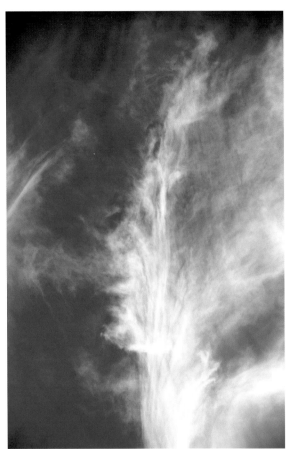

Meditation:

Keep your head up even in bad times.

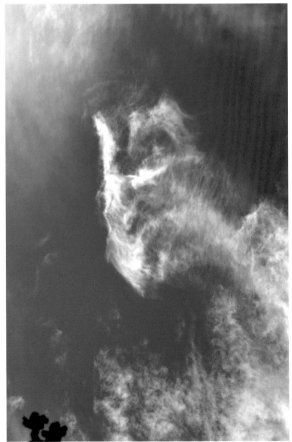

Meditation:

Listen carefully to your mind and body.

Meditation:

Don't mimic others — be your own person.

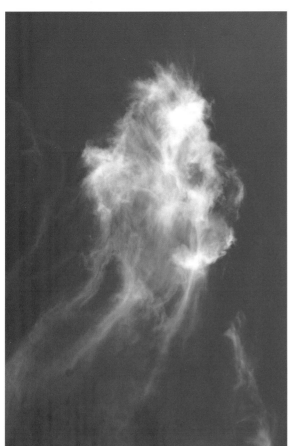

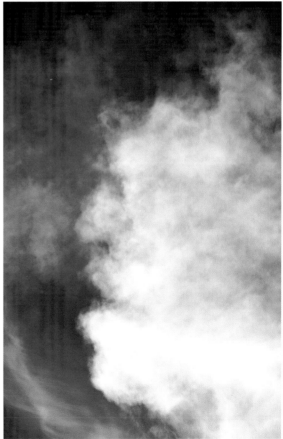

Meditation:

Your task is to set goals
and then meet them each day.

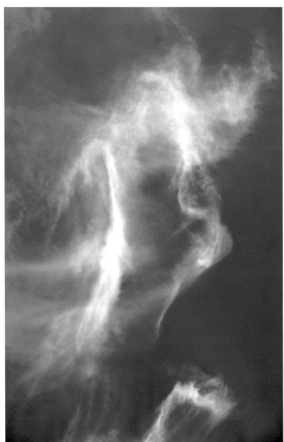

Meditation:

Being alone does not mean
you have to be lonely.

Meditation:

Remember you are beautiful
no matter what you look like.

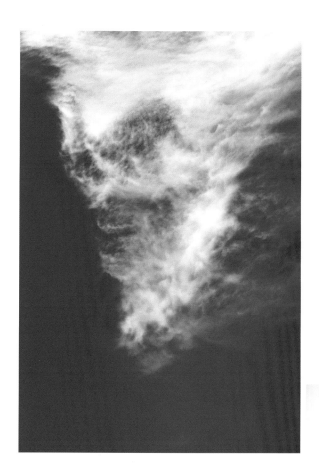

Meditation:

Be vigilent, alert, and ready to act
when needed.

Meditation:

Don't make fun of others,
as it is very hurtful and demeans yourself.

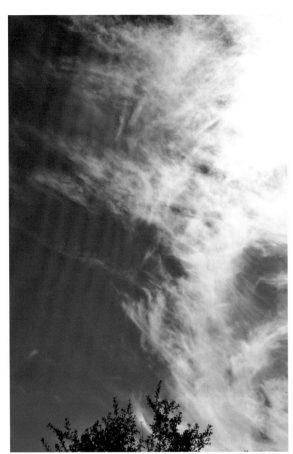

Meditation:

Use discernment in all things you do.

Meditation:

If something does not feel right,
follow your intuition.

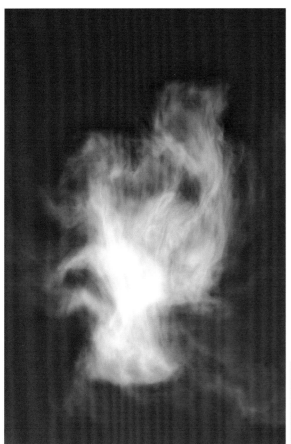

Meditation:

If you are going to be impatient with others,
do the job yourself.

Meditation:

Remember what you share with others
will be shared over and over again.

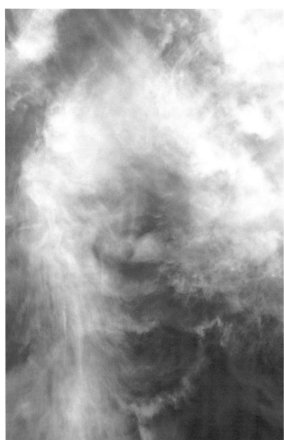

Meditation:

There is a time to be funny.
Bring joy to your life.

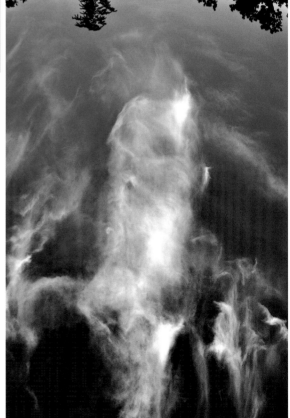

Meditation:

Take responsibility
for all that you think and do.

Meditation:

Listen carefully to what others say and what they mean.

Meditation:

There are always two or more ways to act or do something.

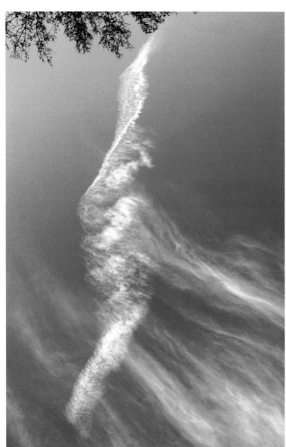

Meditation:

Be proud of who you are.

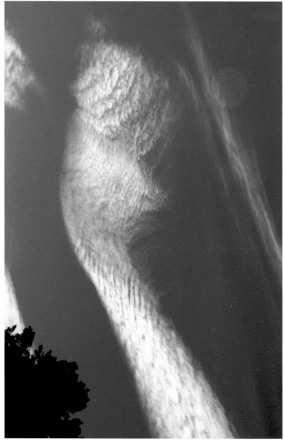

Meditation:

Just because you fear something,
that should not stop you.

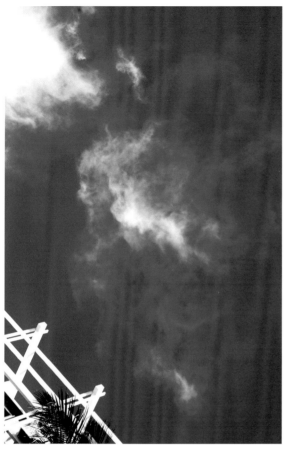

Meditation:

Togetherness is Love.

Meditation:

In your mind, fly high in the sky
and remove yourself from your troubles.

Meditation:

Your wings are made to fly, so do it.

Meditation:

Trust that you will always have
what you need in life.

Meditation:

You may not have all the answers,
but the journey is to seek them.

Meditation:

Beauty comes in so many forms —
open your mind to what beauty is.

Meditation:

Don't have a big head — have humility.

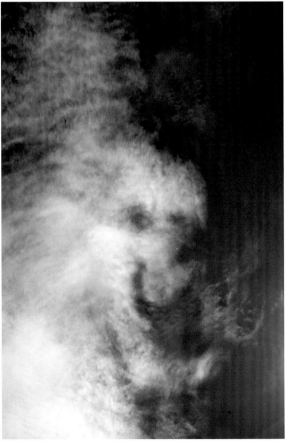

Meditation:

Be the example for others to follow.

Meditation:

When an opportunity comes your way,
remember that you may not get another chance.

Meditation:

Be calm and peaceful in all that you do.

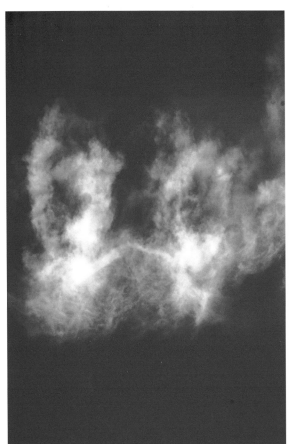

Meditation:

Holding hands and hugging are the best ways to show your caring and love.

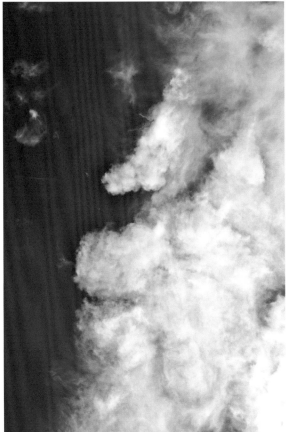

Meditation:

Abundance and prosperity are not solely based on the amount of money you have.

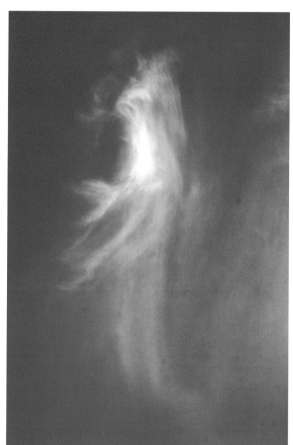

Meditation:

Don't be the Why-Me person
when your troubles may be nothing
when compared to others.

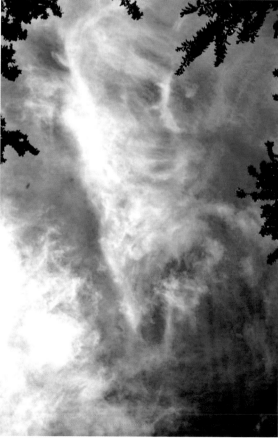

Meditation:

Show your zest for life each and every day.

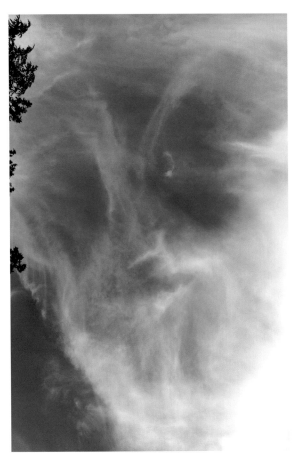

Meditation:

Be careful with others you associate with, as they are a reflection of you.

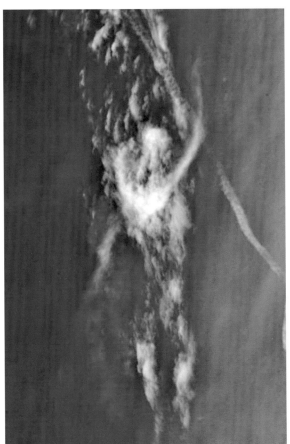

Meditation:

Reach for the sky and stretch your potential.

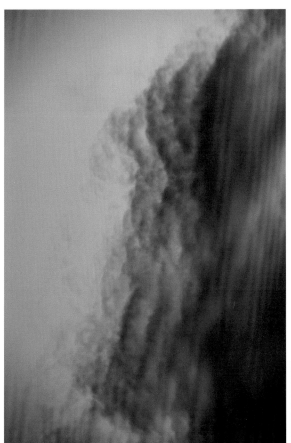

Meditation:

Don't be lost in the crowd —
make sure you are heard and seen.

Meditation:

You are a stand-out among others.

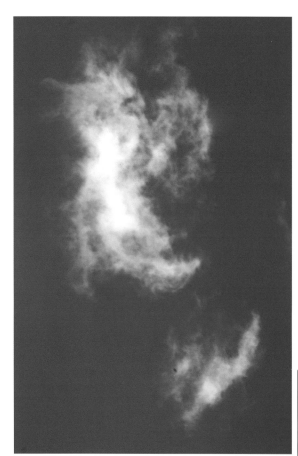

Meditation:

Don't be a baby — whatever has happened before, you must let it go.

Meditation:

Be sure to breathe deeply each day
and take in the benefits to your body.

Meditation:

Compassion for others is key
to spiritual health.

Meditation:

Don't look down on others —
instead, help them to look up.

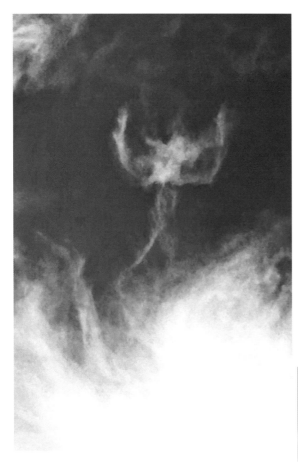

Meditation:

Don't give up – be patient and persistent and things will work out.

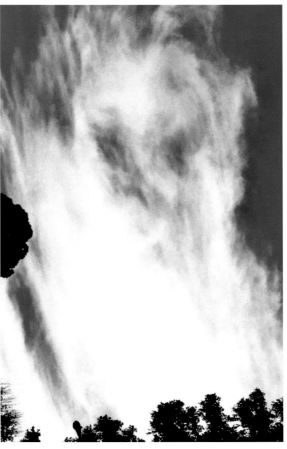

Meditation:

If you are in a bad mood, use your mind to think of things to change it.

Meditation:

Pole vault over any obstacles in your life —
no obstacle is too high.

Meditation:

Meditate today while playing
your favorite music.

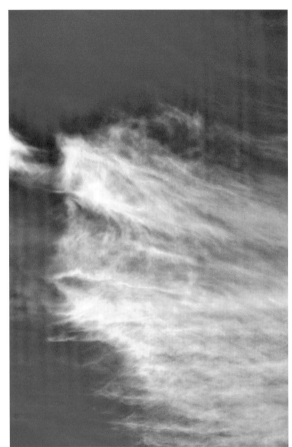

Meditation:

Being serious all the time may not be healthy.

Meditation:

Express your Love to as many people that you can each day.

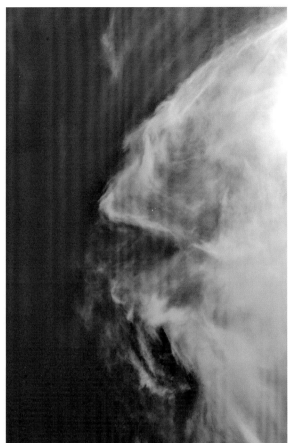

Meditation:

Many people are more successful without having a big mouth.

Meditation:

Your Soul needs to be fed Love, Happiness, Joy, and Peace.

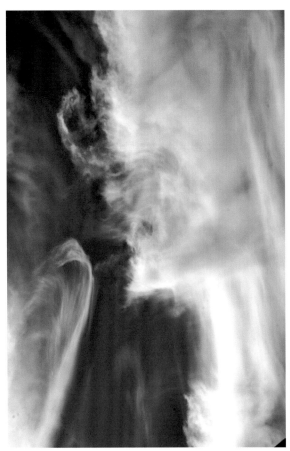

Meditation:

Some people say Who Me
rather than take action themselves.

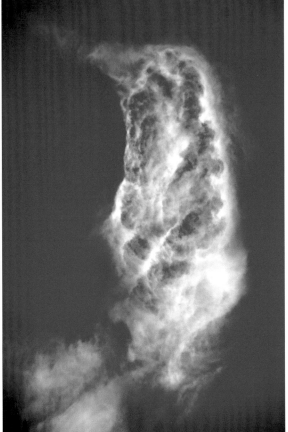

Meditation:

There are many ways to bring passion
into your life each day.

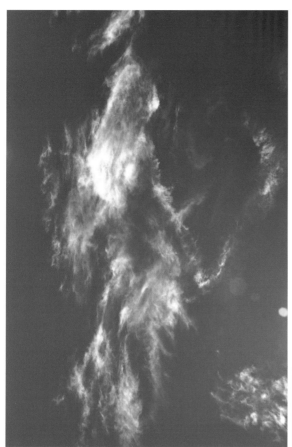

Meditation:

Sometimes you just need to stay home and enjoy yourself in solitude.

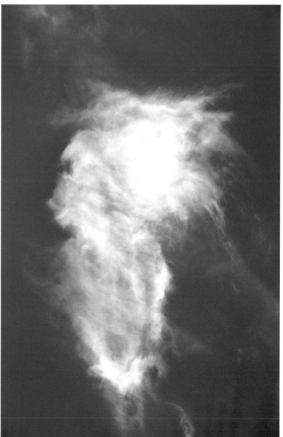

Meditation:

Be still and focus on your life.

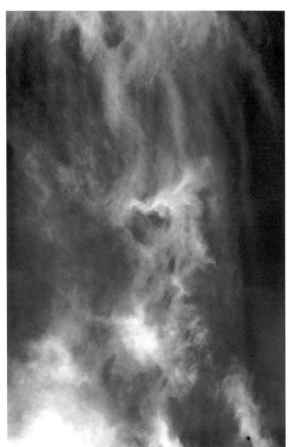

Meditation:

Even a small heart is more powerful
than all the armies of the world.

Meditation:

A smile is the best medicine
for your body and Soul.

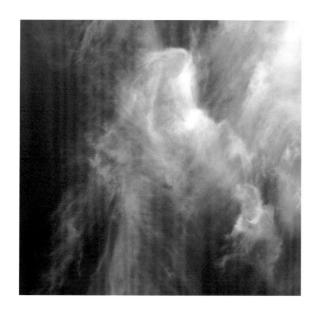

Meditation:

An animal like a dog or cat can be
your very best friend and bring you love.

Meditation:

Keep focused on what is important.

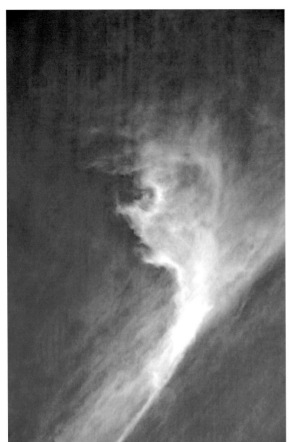

Meditation:

Spend time with yourself each day.

Meditation:

Be open to new ideas and opportunities.

Meditation:

Make sure you see things clearly
before making a decision.

Meditation:

Don't wander aimlessly through life —
make a plan with goal.

Meditation:

Remember to fill your life with happiness and joy.

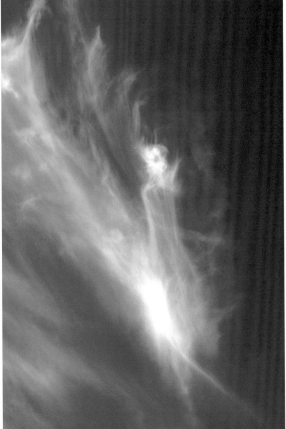

Meditation:

Prayer and Meditation are important to have in your life.

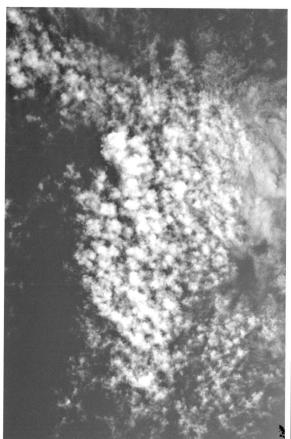

Meditation:

It is a good thing to become invisible in a crowd sometimes.

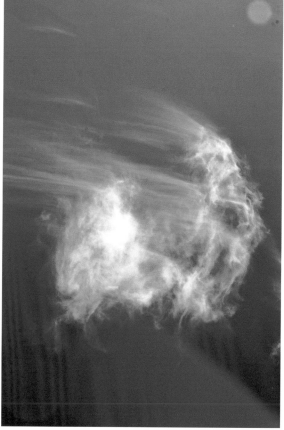

Meditation:

Run away from those who would take advantage of you.

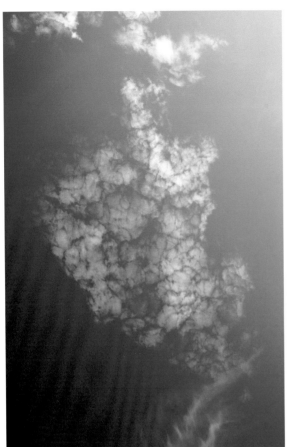

Meditation:

You might consider bowing your head to honor in gratitude for all you have.

Meditation:

Be catlike and be patient before you leap.

Meditation:

Stand tall and firm in your resolve.

Meditation:

Be flexible in your daily life.

Meditation:

It is not necessary to get into someone's face to make your point.

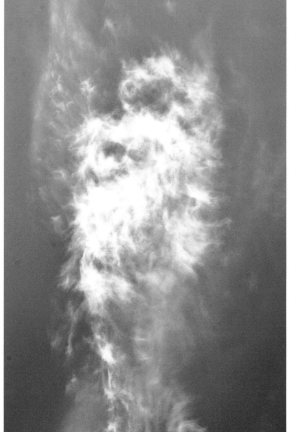

Meditation:

Be inquisitive so that you learn new things each day.

Meditation:

Open your eyes to all that is around you.

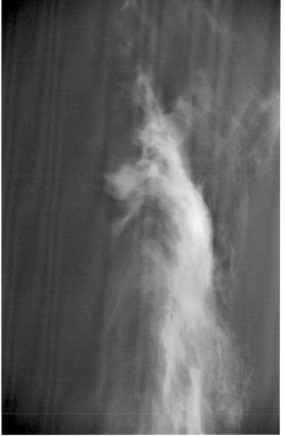

Meditation:

Just be in the moment.

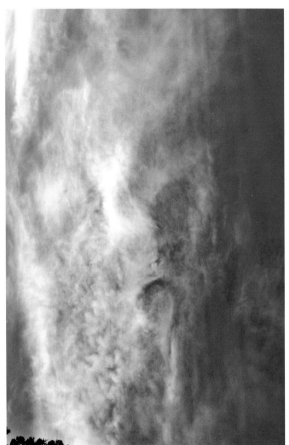

Meditation:

It is okay to be tired and to rest to rejuvenate your mind and body.

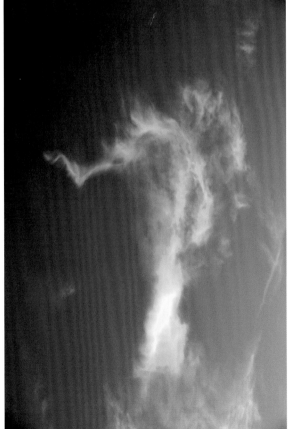

Meditation:

Push away from others who may want to harm you.

Meditation:

Remember your Angels are always around you.

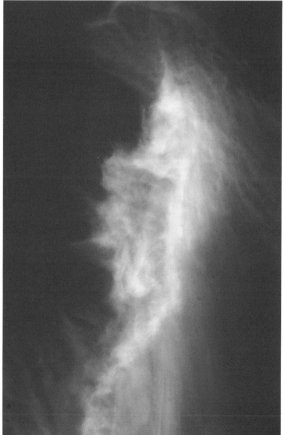

Meditation:

Honor life in all forms
no matter the appearance.

Meditation:

Sometimes you must show your resolve and strength.

Meditation:

Meditate for Peace within yourself and for the World.

Meditation:

Focus each day.

Meditation:

Don't let anyone bully you.

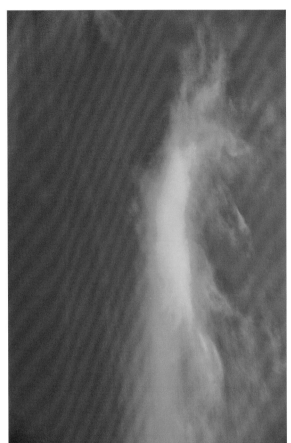

Meditation:

Stand tall and strive to meet your goals.

Meditation:

Don't let your life be a cluttered mess.

Meditation:

Just observe and take in all
that is around you.

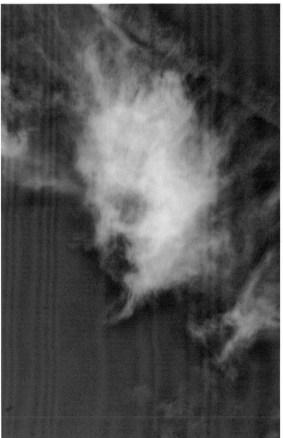

Meditation:

Sometimes you might not feel good,
so this is a time to think positively.

Meditation:

Make sure you bring Joy into your life.

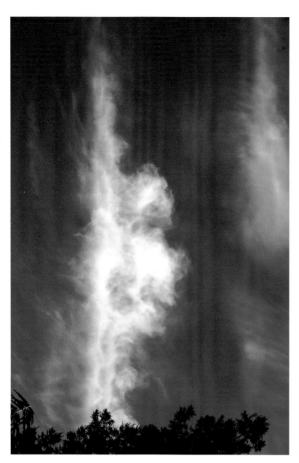

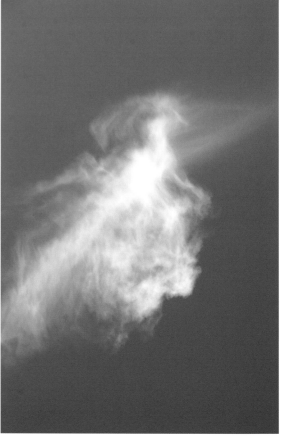

Meditation:

Find the Love that is in your Heart.

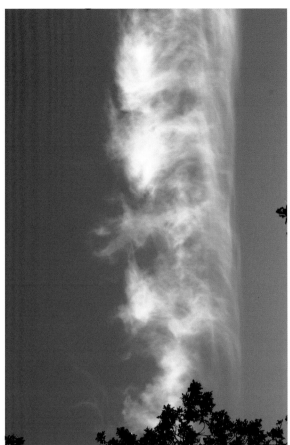

Meditation:

Think of a Totem of Love, Happiness, Joy, and Peace.

Meditation:

Someone might be bigger than you, but that does not make them better.

Meditation:

In our busy world, it is okay to just hide for a while to seek quiet and Peace.

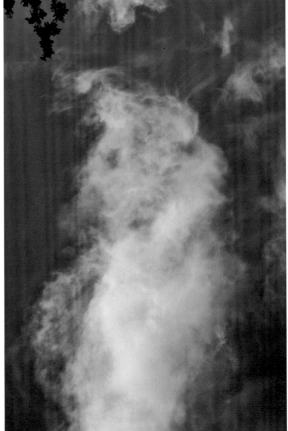

Meditation:

Some days it might be advised to be alone and be a friend to yourself.

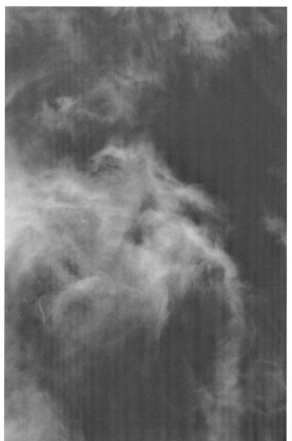

Meditation:

There are times of sadness for each of us, but make sure to take care of yourself.

Meditation:

Make connections with your Angels and Guides.

Meditation:

Let your Angels point the way for you.

Meditation:

Know that you have courage, strength, and Love.

Meditation:

Don't walk into situations you know nothing about – educate yourself first.

Meditation:

Make sure your friends have the qualities of friendship.

Meditation: Rise above your troubles and face them with the strength of the eagle.

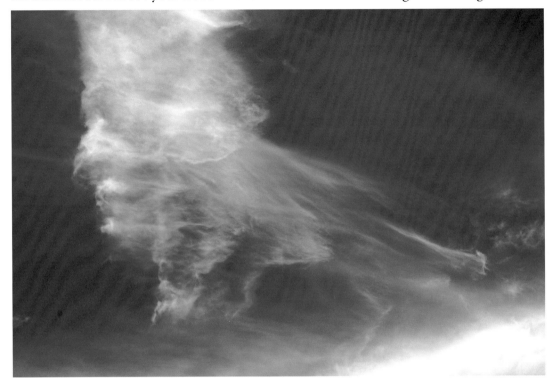

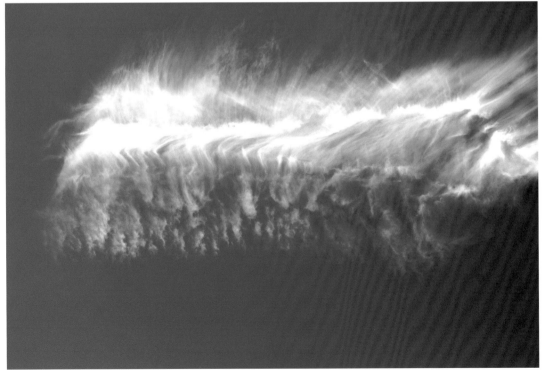

Meditation: You might be slow like the caterpillar but you can still meet your goals.

Meditation: Be positive like the sunlight and reflect away all negativity.

Meditation: All things are possible if you think that they are.

Meditation: See the world around you and use your discretion wisely.

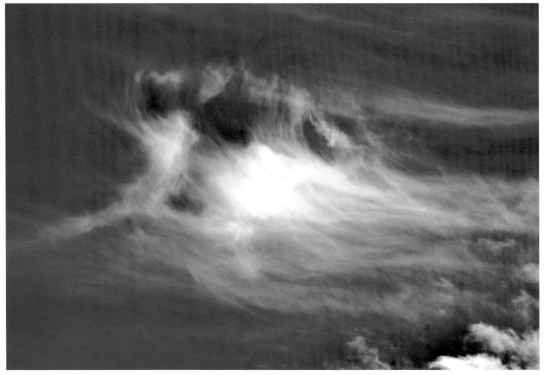

Meditation: Be the rainbow in someone's life.

Meditation: If clouds can have a smile, so can you.

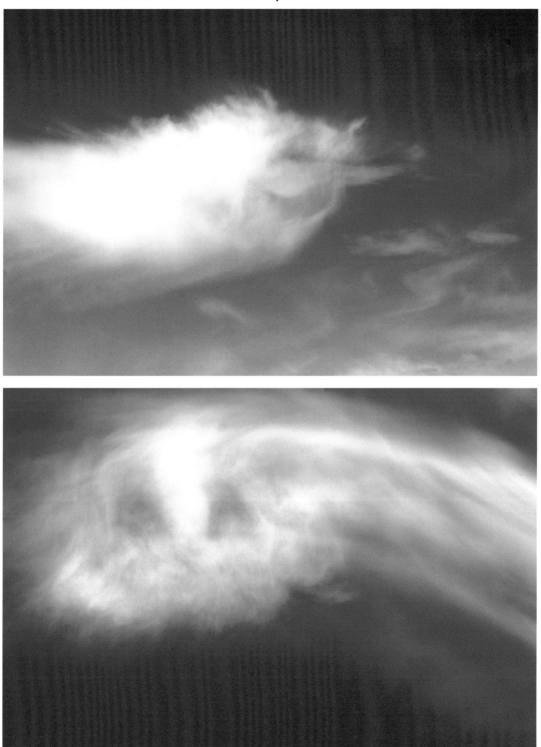

Meditation: Remember that your thoughts control what happens in your life.

Meditation: Don't give away your energy to others — protect it.

Meditation: Positive thoughts and actions bring more positive energies to you.

Meditation: Remember that your life is a Blessing — use it wisely.

Meditation: Don't be surprised to learn that you can make a difference in your life and others.

The Spirit of Peace

Angels of Love

Intuitive and Psychic Resources

I have spent the last 16 years seeking advice and information from a variety of intuitive people such as psychics, intuitive, and tarot card readers, numerologists, and astrological experts. Over the years, I have found several people that I trust because their information and predictions have been incredibly accurate. They are able to gain information from a variety of resources such as my Guides, or their Guides, from Angels and Archangels, and from other Higher Beings.

I have asked them to provide their background, the level of services they provide, and their contact information should you choose to seek their advice.

You will also find that I mention them by their first name in many of the stories in this book. This list below will help you understand who they are when I mention them.

Alan Walden

Tom met Alan in 2009 when he came to a book show in San Francisco. He tapped me on the shoulder as I was standing by my exhibit. He said he had driven for four hours from Mt. Shasta to meet me. I was wondering who this was. After we started talking, a visible bubble formed around us as protection. We talked for an hour standing up. At that moment, I learned that Alan was a very intuitive person. One of the things he told me is that I have to go to Australia as I had previous lives there as an Aboriginal tribesman 5,000 years ago. While I thought that was strange, Caroline and I did go to Australia in 2015 to visit the Uluru Sacred Site and more. He was so right.

Whenever we go to San Francisco, we make it a point to meet with Alan. Each time, he channels important information from "Above" to us. It is always amazing and enlightening.

Alan has created Shasta Art. His art flows from the Angels and other Higher Beings. He expresses his innermost feelings through his art. He has always sought out spiritual knowledge and spiritual connections. Each piece of art is different, but a common theme that emanates from all is the Heart. At the core of our Heart/Soul is Love, which he feels sends out vibrating healing. Alan believes that the true essence of our higher self and all that is good within us allows us to express beauty.

Check out his website and art at: http://shastaart.weebly.com/

Brook Rivera

Brook came into our lives in 2007 one month prior to our trip to Peru. She became a vital resource to us in many ways. We could not have traveled to various parts of the world without her taking care of our animals and home. Therefore she allowed us the freedom to evolve on our spiritual journey. Brook is a very loving and spiritual person with her own intuitive skills. She is also trained in nutrition, and the effects of foods on the human body and spirit.

Emerald Alurin Stara

Intuitive Consultant

Emerald Alurin Stara is an Intuitive Consultant and the published author/illustrator of "Princess Crystallina and the Star Children."

Emerald offers Oracle Tarot Card Readings to her clients, a spirit-based method of inquiry for wisdom, insight and understanding. Her unique interactive style combines extensive knowledge, including Numerology, with personal attunement through her clairsensient, clairvoyant, and clairaudient abilities.

Emerald may be contacted by email or phone:
Email: emstara@yahoo.com
Phone: 530.274.3398 and 530.388.0557

Francie Marie

Francie Marie is a psychic based in Northern California.

She can be contacted by either email or phone:
Email: fmw3333@yahoo.com
Phone: 530.613.3679

Jaap van Etten

Jaap van Etten, PhD, was born and educated in The Netherlands. He received his PhD in Biology in Amsterdam, specializing in ecology. For the past twenty six years, his focus has been on metaphysical ecology. He studies and teaches about human energies, Earth energies, energies of stones, crystals and crystal skulls, cosmic energies, and how these energies interact.

Jaap is trained in many healing modalities. He has the ability to read energies of those he works with. This helps him to establish a good picture of the issues a person is dealing with. He is specialized in working with entities, both in detecting and removing them. He clears houses and land from negative energies and gives advices on the best location for any construction on your property.

Jaap is an internationally known speaker, workshop facilitator, healer, and author. He has worked in many countries all over the world.

He is the author of *Gifts of Mother Earth,* a book that describes the interactions between human energies and the energies of the Earth. He also is the author of two books on crystal skulls. These books describe how these ancient and contemporary tools support us on our journey of remembering and fully becoming our true selves. His fourth book focuses on the Birth of a new consciousness.

Since 1998, he has lived in the United States with his wife Jeanne Michaels, and currently resides in the Sedona area, Arizona.

Jaap may be contacted by email, website, or phone:
Email address: jaap@lemurantis.com
Website: http://www.lemurantis.com
Phone: 928.707.9873

Judith M. McLean, PhD

Judith provides services such as: aura reading, health scans, intuitive readings, aura clearings, help with spirit releasement and other dimensional scanning, past life readings.

She can be contacted at:
Phone: 717.762.2166
Email: Sanctuary11@comcast.net

Kathleen Scott

Kathleen Scott is a retired Massage Therapist who now educates people on how to use Young Living essential oils. Kathleen teaches classes in Raindrop Technique, Digestive Raindrop, Neuro-Auricular Technique, as well as Healing Sound Classes. In addition Kathleen can teach the 18-layer Chakra and Auric cleanse which was a gift from four Archangels.

Kathleen can be contracted by Email at skatzz@aol.com

Kerry Jehanne

I am a practitioner of multidimensional healing modalities with a deep passion for my work and tender compassion for my clients. I help individuals and groups experience a vibrational shift towards a healthier and more harmonious state of being by applying various innovative methods that promote physical, mental, and emotional wellness as well as spiritual integration.

My healing practice started as a result of my own journey through some treacherous times. As I felt more and more gratitude for my new life, and all the wonderful people and Divine beings that helped me create it, my purpose started to awaken in me. My life purpose, to help others, arose from the integration of this profound gratitude. I was inspired to offer the same successful healing modalities that transformed my life.

I use a system of healing that operates at the level of consciousness, where everything is viewed as information and vibrational frequencies that are interconnected by and are coherently organized within a unified field. My intentional alignment with this field allows me to help my clients facilitate the restorative shifts necessary for optimal physical, mental, emotional and spiritual well-being. My work is guided and supported by many other-dimensional beings that assist humanity in frequency ascension.

For more information, please contact me at:
Phone: 916.704.0412
Email: kerryjehanne@gmail.com
Website: http://www.kerryjehanne.com

Linda Schooler

Linda is a Clairvoyant Consultant who gives readings in person and by phone.

She can be contacted at www.LindaSchooler.com

Mandy Milovich

Reiki Master Certified Massage Therapist, Mother of Four

I remember entering the home of a lady that I now know as my friend... The Buddha statues and crystals around the home were something that I realized I wanted to have in mine. Her home exuded a wonderful energy and along every wall was a painting that spoke to the very center of my being.

Instantly drawn in, I knew that I had to be connected with this artist. I was mesmerized by the swirls of color that created another communication portal between me and my guides. My "Clair" senses being complimented by this Portal.

I was diligent about meeting he who created these. Being sensitive to energies, I was really taken by surprise that they would affect me so deeply but that does not even come close to the experiences I have had after meeting Tom. Tom Lumbrazo has been a Beacon of Light. I find I get a wonderful healing just being around him. His generosity is unmatched.

I was truly blessed to manifest his amazing art around the store but to gain him as a friend...words can't describe.

Tom is now the only artist that I carry in my store Positive Practice.

Positive Practice has a mission. A mission to provide a place where everyone is welcome to explore our vast selection of quality merchandise from around the world. We strive to be a valuable community resource for healing. Our practitioners and services seek to inspire, encourage, and celebrate those desiring to grow in recovery, faith, and spiritual awakening.

Whatever your path; come in and enjoy the shop's great visual experience and feel the energy.

Mandy may be contacted by website, at her shop, or by phone:
Positive Practice
2721 Fulton Avenue
Sacramento, CA 95821
Website: http://www. positivepracticestore.com
Phone: 916.973.9983

It Is Our Destiny to Be Stewards of the Planet Earth!

Wisdom

With Love and Protection, Our Partners and Ourselves Are Not Looking Back...Only Forward....

Caroline

Tom

Blackie

Slim